RICHARD'S BICYCLE BOOK

Richard Ballantine
Illustrated by John Batchelor

Ballantine Books · New York

This book is dedicated to
Samuel Joseph Melville, hero.

SBN 345-22813-8-195

First Printing: October, 1972
Second Printing: November, 1972
Third Printing: March, 1973
Fourth Printing: June, 1973
Fifth Printing: December, 1973

Printed in the United States of America

Ballantine Books, Inc.
201 East 50th Street, New York, N.Y. 10022

Layout and make-up Mike Jarvis

Contents

BOOK 1

BOOK 2

Book One

Get a Bike!

Bicycle shops are capitalizing on today's version of the 1849 California gold rush. Sales in 1971 were 8.5 million bikes worth $500 million, double the number sold in 1960, and in 1972 bikes should outsell cars. Most active stores are able to sell out a shipment of bikes within 2 to 3 weeks. Manufacturers are 3 to 5 months behind orders. Bikes are everywhere and all kinds of people—63 million—use them. Hertz is even considering a nation-wide system of rental bikes. This tremendous boom owes a great deal to the evolution and improvement of bicycles and to changes in the American scene.

The typical pre-World War II American bike was sturdy but cumbersome. Equipped with a single pedal operated coaster brake and one low, slow gear, these "balloon tire bombers" hit the scales at 60 to 75 pounds. Used primarily by youngsters not old enough to drive, they were workhorse machines tough enough to withstand jolting rides over curbs and through fields, frequent nights out in the rain, and a generally high level of abuse. Fond nostalgia permeates memories of these bikes, but for the most part only people who had no other alternative used them.

Rover Safety – 1885

After World War II returning G.I.'s brought home samples of a new kind of bike with a thinner frame and wheels, dual hand-operated caliper brakes, and 3-speed gears. Dubbed an "English racer" because of its startlingly better performance, this is actually the "tourist" bike, the common European machine for local use to and from work, shopping, mail delivery, police work, and the like. Light weight (45 pounds) and geared for both flats and hills, the tourist bike is much easier to ride. A hit with the younger set as improved basic transportation, it provided the foundation for bicycling as an adult recreation in the U.S. of A. In the late '50s and early '60s stores devoted mainly to the sale and rental of bicycles developed steadily. Americans began spending more of their increased free time on afternoon rides in the countryside or parks. Bikes appeared in force on university campuses, and hardier souls began using them as all around transportation.

In the 1960s came the 10- and 15-speed racing-touring bikes. If the tourist bike is much better than a balloon tire bomber, the racing bike is incomparably so. Weighing about 22 pounds, they move much faster and more easily than other types of bikes. The first models came from Europe, where bike races are more important than baseball is here, and short supply made them very expensive. But adults have the economic clout to buy what they want, and while in 1965-66 only 20% of the bikes sold were adult machines, now they account for 65% of the market. High sales volume has lowered prices, so that a serviceable tourist model is about $40, with better quality machines up to $90. Ten- and 15-speed models run about $60 for a cheapie, $120 for a good quality bike, and $250 and more for a really high quality machine.

A list of all the vastly expanded applications and uses for light-weight bikes would be dull. But the main advantages are:

Economics

With even moderate use a bike will pay for itself. Suppose you use a bike instead of public transportation or a car to get to work and back. Figure public transportation at $1.00 a day. Say it rains once a week and you live in the Northeast with an 8 month bike season. That's 4 days × 4 weeks × 8 months × $1 or $128 which buys a very nice bike. In sunnier climes with an 11 month season ring up $220. On a 20 mile round trip @ .12 a mile a car is into it for $2.40 a day, or $300 to $500 a year. Many bikes sold today are guaranteed parts and labor for three years and will last a great deal longer.

Getting to and from work is just one application. Bikes are just dandy for visiting friends, light shopping, nipping down to the movies and the like. You save money every time. Besides easing many of your chores and tasks, bikes are worthwhile in and of themselves, so that a bike easily "pays for itself" in rides taken just for fun and pleasure.

Convenience

Speed. In heavy traffic you can expect to average 10 mph, and in lighter traffic 15 mph. I regularly ride $2\frac{1}{2}$ miles to midtown Manhattan from my apartment on the lower east side in 15 minutes, usually less. The bus takes at least 30 to 40 minutes, the subway about 25 to 35. When I first got into bikes it used to be my delight to race subway-travelling friends from 120th street to Greenwich Village – about 6 to 7 miles – and beat them. There have been bike versus bus, subway, and/or sports car contests in many cities, and in each case I know about the bike has always won.

One reason a bike is so fast is that it can wiggle through the traffic jams that now typify American cities and towns. Another is the fact that a bike is door-to-door. Use of public transportation involves walking to the local stop, waiting around for the bus or train, possibly a transfer with another wait, and then a walk from the final stop to your destination. Cars have to be parked. On a bike you simply step out the door and take off. No waiting, no parking problems.

The bike's capabilities make it a real freedom machine. Your lunch hour: tired of the same company cafeteria slop or local hash joint? Getting to a new and interesting restaurant a mile or so away is a matter of minutes. Lots of errands to do? A bike can nip from one place to another much faster than you can hoof it, and has a car beat all hollow in traffic and for parking. What might ordinarily take an hour is only 15 minutes on the bike. And if there is a lot to lug around, it is the bike and not you that does the work. Last minute decision to catch a film? Boom! Ten minutes and you're there before the subway even got going. If, like me, you are at all nocturnal, a bike is a tremendous advantage. Subways and buses tend to become elusive or disappear altogether as the wee hours approach. There is also a powerful contrast between a journey on a grubby, dirty, and noisy (to the point where your hearing acuity is measurably and permanently diminished) subway or bus where you run a definite risk of being mugged or raped, and a graceful, rhythmic ride in which you glide through calm and silent streets or through the stillness of a country night under the moon and stars.

Medical

All right, you say. So it takes less time than the subway. But I've got to work for a living and the subway is easier, takes less out of me. You expect me to get up in the morning and crack off 10 miles? Finish a day of hard work and do another 10? I'd never make it.

Get this. Even a moderate amount of exercise makes life *easier*. It gives your body tone and bounce which makes daily work and chores a breeze. Simply put, this is because exercise increases your range of possible effort, putting daily activities towards the center rather than the peak of your capabilities. So as you go through the day you are just cruising. It's something like the difference between a 25- and 100-horsepower automobile engine. At 60 mph the 25 horse is working hard but the 100 is just loafing. It is important to realize that you can get this increased bounce, verve, and good feeling with relatively little time and effort. Bicycling will make your work and day easier, not harder.

Are you familiar with "cleaning out" a motor vehicle? Cars today often operate in stop and go traffic for long periods of time. The engine becomes clogged with carbon and other residue. The car stumbles and staggers, it works harder than it needs to, and gas consumption goes up. The best thing for any such car is to be taken out on a highway and run fast, for at higher speeds the engine cleans itself out. Your body is a machine with exactly similar characteristics, and you will literally become more fagged out and tired just sitting still than if you run around the block a few times.

According to Eugene Sloane in his *Complete Book of Bicycling*, if you get in some sort of regular exercise you can expect:

to live for up to five years longer;

think better (more blood to the brain – and if you think this is crazy go out and run around for a while and then think it through again);

sleep better, and in general be more relaxed;

be stronger and more resistant to injury;

reduce the incidence of degenerative vascular diseases responsible for or associated with heart attacks, strokes, and high blood pressure.

As cardiovascular problems account for over 50% of all deaths in the U.S. of A. each year this last point is worth some elaboration. The basic deal with the cardiovascular system is movement, the flow of blood through your heart, veins, arteries, and so forth. The heart normally pumps about 5 quarts per minute, and during exercise up to 30 quarts per minute. If this flow is sluggish and slow, the system clogs up. In arteriosclerosis, for example, the walls of the system become hardened and calcified. This decreases the bore of the arteries and veins, resulting in a diminished capacity to carry blood. The heart must therefore pump harder and higher blood pressure results. High blood pressure is a cause of stroke or rupture of brain blood vessels. Arteriosclerosis happens to everybody, but extent is governed by the rate of flow of the blood. Exercise stimulates the blood flow, and does not permit calcification to occur as rapidly.

Atherosclerosis is a related malady. This is when fatty substances are deposited on the lining of the blood vessels. Clots in the blood may be formed as a result, and these can jam up the system at critical points such as the brain or heart, causing stroke or heart attack. Again, exercise by stimulating the blood flow helps prevent fatty deposits.

So, the main benefits of regular exercise are first, that it will help keep your blood circulatory system cleaned out; secondly, the heart muscle, like any other, responds to exercise by becoming larger and more efficient, so that each heartbeat delivers more oxygen to the body; and thirdly, lung-filling capacity is restored or enlarged. In short, you can do more, and recover more quickly from doing it.

Bicycling in particular is a complete exercise. Not only are the legs, the body's largest accessory blood pumping mechanism, used extensively, but also arm, shoulder, back, abdominal, and diaphragmatic muscles. At the same time there is enough flexibility so that muscle groups can be worked individually, and of course pace can be set to suit the rider.

A word about weight control. Bicycling or other exercise will help your body's tone and figure. But for weight loss eat less food. A brisk ride does not entitle you to apple pie and ice cream. Regular cycling burns off about 300 calories per hour and hill climbing or racing about 600 per hour. Your body uses up about 150 calories per hour anyhow, and so in the case of regular cycling this means a burn off of an extra 150 calories per hour. At 3600 calories per pound, it would take 24 hours of riding to lose this amount. It's much simpler to just eat less. Curiously enough, cycling may help you to do this. Regular exercise can change the metabolic balance of the body and restore normal automatic appetite control so that you eat no more than you actually need.

A serious health hazard for the urban cyclist is hyperventilation of highly polluted air. See Traffic Jamming for more information on this subject.

Ecology

Our country is literally drowning in pollutants and many of them come from transportation machinery. In the cities the internal combustion engine is a prime offender, contributing not only up to 85% of all air pollution,* but of an especially noxious quality. The effluents from gasoline engines hang in the air and chemically interact with other substances and sunlight to form even deadlier poisons. Living in a major city is the same thing as smoking two packs of cigarettes a day.**

All city transportation contributes to pollution. Subways run on electricity generated in plants fired by fossil fuels or deadly atomic reactors. But as anyone who has been lucky enough to live through a taxicab strike or vehicle ban knows, cars and buses are the real problem. I shall never forget a winter about 3 or 4 years ago when a friend and I came driving into New York City late at night after a vacation in Canada. To my amazement, the air was perfectly clear. The lights of the city shone like jewels and each building was clear and distinct. From the west bank of the Hudson river I could for the first (and perhaps only) time in my life see Manhattan and the Bronx in perfect detail from beginning to end, and even beyond to Brooklyn and her bridges. As we crossed the George Washington Bridge the air was clean and fresh, and the city, usually an object

*Reinow, L.&L. MOMENT IN THE SUN (Ballantine, New York).
**Commoner, Barry, THE CLOSING CIRCLE (Jonathan Cape, London).

of horror and revulsion, was astoundingly beautiful and iridescent. The explanation was simple: enough snow had fallen to effectively eliminate vehicle traffic for a couple of days. No vehicles, no crap in the air. A better world.

Arguments against motorized transport are usually dismissed as idealistic and impractical and on the grounds that the time-saving

characteristics of such vehicles are essential. The fact is that even pedestrians are easily able to drone past most traffic, and of course bicycles can do even better. A saving in physical effort is realized, but few of us are healthy enough to (a) need this, or (b) dismiss inhaling the poisons (equivalent to two packs of cigarettes a day) which necessarily accompany the internal combustion engine.

Walking, roller skating, or riding a bicycle is an efficient use of energy and reduces wastage. Utilizing a 300 horsepower, 5000 pound behemoth to move one single 150 pound person a few miles is like using an atomic bomb to kill a canary. The U.S. of A. is unique in its ability to consume and waste. In fact, we utilize something like 60% of the world's resources for the benefit of about 7% of her population. For example, we import fish meal from South American countries where people are starving, to feed to our beef herds, and then wonder why people down there don't like us. Using a bicycle is a starting antidote to the horrors of U.S. of A. consumerism.

Which brings us to the most positive series of reasons for trying to use bicycles at every opportunity. Basically, this is that it will enhance your life, bringing to it an increase in quality of experience which will find its reflection in everything you do.

Well! you have to expect that I would believe bicycling is a good idea, but how do I get off expressing the notion that bicyling is philosophically and morally sound? Because it is something that *you do*, not something that is done to you. Need I chronicle the oft-cited concept of increasing alienation in American life? The mechanization of work and daily activities, the hardships our industrial society places in the way of loving and fulfilling relationships and family life, the tremendous difficulties individuals experience trying to influence political and economic decisions which affect them and others?

Of course there will always be people who say that they like things the way they are. They find the subway really interesting, or insist on driving a chrome bomb and rattling everybody's windows. But the fact is that subways are crowded, dirty, impersonal, and *noisy*, and nearly all cars are ego-structured worthless tin crap junk (with bikes the more you pay the less you get).

The most important effect of mechanical contraptions is that they defeat consciousness. Consciousness, self-awareness, and development are the prerequisites for a life worth living. Now look at what happens to you on a bicycle. It's immediate and direct. *You* pedal. *You* make decisions. *You* experience the tang of the air and the surge of power as you bite into the road. You're vitalized. As you hum along you fully and gloriously experience the day, the sunshine, the clouds, the breezes. You're alive! You are going someplace, and it is *you* who is doing it. Awareness increases, and each day becomes a little more important to you. With increased awareness you see and notice more, and this further reinforces awareness.

Each time you insert *you* into a situation, each time *you* experience, you fight against alienation and impersonality, you build consciousness and identity. You try to understand things in the ways that are important to you. And these qualities carry over into everything you do.

An increased value on one's own life is the first step in social conscience and politics. Because to you life is dear and important and fun, you are much more easily able to understand why this is also true for a Vietnamese, a black, or a Tobago islander. Believe it. The salvation of the world is the development of personality and identity for everybody in it. Much work, many lifetimes. But a good start for you is *Get a bicycle!*

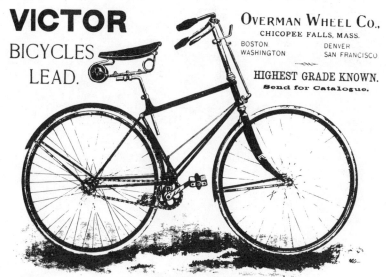

VICTOR SAFETY BICYCLE. – MODEL B.

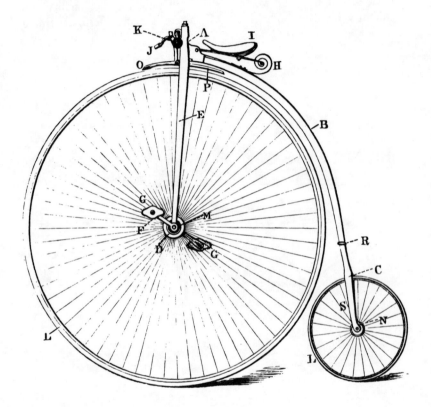

2. Choosing Mounts

What kind of bike for you? The main points are covered here, but you should also look over the sections on riding, fitting, touring, and racing to get the best idea of what's going on and what your particular needs may be before arriving at a final selection. This chapter is broken down into three parts: adult bicycles; children's bicycles; and other. Technical information given for adult bicycles applies to any bicycle and will not be repeated in each section.

Adult Bicycles

I hope your decision will be to get a 10-speed bicycle. They can be set up to suit nearly any rider, job, or purpose, are dynamic, responsive, and vibrant, the most comfortable, and give the most speed for the least effort so that you will get more out of riding and will be encouraged to do even more. They are also the easiest to service. Initial cost may seem high, but experience has shown that most people who start with a balloon heavyweight or 3-speed tourist model soon find themselves desiring (and acquiring) a racing bike. It takes no longer than the first time such a machine sweeps by them going up a hill. Although initial cost is higher my advice is to *save your money* and get a racing bike in the first place. More importantly, you get the most fun and turn-on for your dollar, and you get it right away.

Bicycle categories by function are traditionally three: a balloon bomber for really tough work like riding on beaches and fields, newspaper delivery, collisions, and absolutely no care; a 3-speed tourist model for utility use such as local errands, shopping, lots of stop-and-go riding, short trips, good durability, and minimal maintenance; a 10-speed for longer trips (over 25 miles), touring, racing, hilly terrain, durability dependent on model, and moderate maintenance. Actually, a 10-speed can be set up for almost any purpose or job except beach riding. The same machine, with minor modifications, can compete in a race, go on a camping tour, and haul groceries or newspapers. It can even (ugh!) pull a trailer. The only crucial difference is the method of operation for the gears: the 3-speed can be shifted to the correct gear at any time, the 10-speed must be shifted while the bicycle is in motion. It's easy once you get the knack, and the 10-speed's efficiency outweighs the disadvantage of initial unfamiliarity. If you get stopped in a "wrong" (inefficient) gear, it is easy to shift once you are under way again.

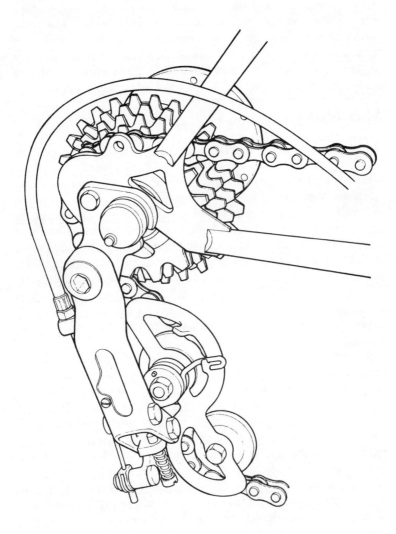

Rear derailleur and freewheel for a 10-speed bike.

The question of durability is largely a function of bicycle model and weight and rider sense. Ten-speeds range from ultra-light (20 pounds) alloy models to heavy (35 pounds) steel models. My first 10-speed was a sturdy machine with steel wheels which I not only rode hard and fast over bumpy streets, but also used for games of bicycle tag in the woods and fields, as well as just plain cross-country and back-trail riding. It held up just fine.

The classic down-swept handlebars of the 10-speed are not a requirement; you can equip or buy such a bike with conventional tourist handlebars, although it wouldn't be to your advantage to do so (more on handlebars later). With the exception of the cheaper models, 10-speed bikes have the much better center-pull caliper brakes, rather than the coaster or side-pull caliper brakes usually supplied with 3-speed bikes. Comfort is sometimes cited in favor of the 3-speed. The fact is that the 10-speed has a wider variety of riding positions, allows you to utilize more muscles to greater advantage, and is therefore much less tiring to ride than a 3-speed.

The choice of bike is therefore largely governed by the type of person you are and how heavy you want to get into bicycling, the contents of your pocketbook, and real-life physical factors such as the quality of your neighborhood and the number of stairs you climb every day. It is the first of these which is the most relevant, and what you must assess is how much consciousness you want to bring to bicycling. Not everybody is interested in the boiling scald of blood through their veins as they sprint up the highway or the eerie desolation of a chill night. Get a 3-speed if: you are not terribly interested in bicycling and just want something you can stick in the shed or basement to use for local jaunts once or twice a month (if you're really in this category and can do so, rent machines); you or the prospective rider are not at all mechanically inclined and don't care to be; you need a knock-around bike for use by several different people or just want a worry-free machine. There is nothing degenerate about this last state of affairs. There are times when I prefer the totally casual spirit of the 3-speed, where one can just drop it on the spot, bash it around, and in general not think about what is going on. But this is the exception, not the rule. Over the long haul, the 10-speed is just so much better, so much more rewarding, that it will surely overcome any diffidence you feel about bicycling and make you an enthusiast.

Expense is a consideration only if your absolute maximum is

$25.00, which restricts you to a serviceable used 3-speed. If you have $35.00 to $45.00 you can buy a used bike that at least has 10 speeds, if nothing else. More on this later.

Most of the more pragmatic considerations in type of bicycle are physical:

For hilly terrain get a 10-speed, no matter what.

RUSHING A RISE.

If you live at the end of a long, rocky dirt road you may want a sturdier model 10-speed. This is also a question of rider weight. For example, I gave a 13-year-old, 100-pound cousin a Peugeot UO-8 two years ago. At 27 pounds this is closer to an ultra-light 20-pound racer than a 35 pound heavyweight. My cousin's family lives at the top of a steep, winding, rocky dirt road about one-eighth of a mile long, and my cousin's idea of fun is to blaze down the hill as fast as he can. The Peugeot is holding up fine, but I am sure that if I tried the same stunt with my 150 pounds' wear and tear on the machine would be noticeably greater. Bear in mind that "sturdier" bikes are built that way because they have to be in order to overcome inherently inferior materials and manufacturing techniques. The amount of extra strength gained is debatable, and only at considerable costs to the power-to-weight ratio. I myself would stick with a lighter machine – and take it easy over the bumps.

Carrying the bicycle is a problem largely confined to stair-climbing apartment dwellers. There's only one answer, and that's a light 10-speed. Folding bikes and 3-speeds run 40-50 pounds. I'm not Charles Atlas, but I'm certainly of average strength or better, and I assure you that the difference between 20 and 45 pounds up two to four flights of stairs is very noticeable. Unless you are particularly athletic or into S & M get a 10-speed.

Using a car or public transportation to get to a departure point for a trip is also part of carrying. Any 10-speed is easier to take apart than a 3-speed, and if your bike is even of minimal quality, it will have quick-release wheels which come off at the flick of a lever. Or it can be equipped with lever-nuts for $2. A folding bike takes up a little less room, true, but folding bikes are worthless (look 'em up in Other), so you lose more than you gain.

Storage is also an issue only for apartment dwellers. Again, although the folding bike takes up less room, in balance the 10-speed wins out. With the wheels off it can be hung in the closet. If you are really cramped hang it from the ceiling or wall via brackets or pulleys. Stick it in the shower stall or bathtub. Look afield. Your building (or one nearby) should have a basement or broom closet or some other niche. You can work something out and under any circumstance will find the 10-speed easier to deal with than the 3-speed.

For frequency of repair the 3-speed has it all over the 10-speed. All the 3-speed hub will need for years is a monthly shot of oil. Once it does go however, it is much too complicated to fix, and most bicycle shops will simply replace it. It is also considerably less efficient than the 10-speed design, and transmits less pedal effort to the rear wheel. The 10-speed, while more efficient, requires more frequent adjustment and servicing. However, because the parts are all quite simple and out in the open where they are easy to get at, this is easy to do. In fact, it is part of the fun of riding. The vitality and responsiveness of the 10-speed is such that you come to enjoy fine-tuning your bike.

Perhaps now you have started to form a notion of what kind of bike you would like to have. But prices vary from $40 to $600 for a bewildering array of bicycles. Here is some technical information to guide you through the maze and help you get your money's worth.

The significant components of a bicycle are the frame, brakes, rims, tires and hubs; gears and gear changing hardware, chainwheel, cranks, and pedals; and stem, handlebars, and saddle.

According to the grade of component selected by the manufacturer, the price for a 3-speed will range from $40 to $100, from $75 to $300 for production line 10-speeds, and $400 and up for custom bikes. Manufacturers tend to assemble rather than manufacture bicycles, getting the components from a number of independent companies. Hence, two bikes in the same price category from two different brand name "manufacturers" sometimes have exactly the same parts.

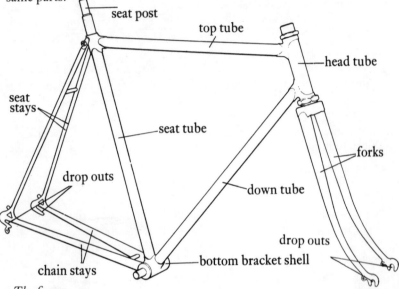

The frame

The frame is the heart and soul of a bicycle. It is the chief determinant of bicycle weight, and the more you pay the lighter the weight for the same strength. Frames are not meant to be rigid or unyielding, but rather to absorb irregularities from the road surface. Called resiliency or twang or flex, this is a function of quality of materials and manufacturing methods, and gives better bikes more springiness and vitality. There is no way to work around a cheap frame. Other components can be modified or changed but the frame endures, and it should be the first focus of your attention when considering a prospective bike.

Inexpensive coaster brake, 3-speed, and cheap 10-speed bikes use seamed tubing, made by wrapping a long, flat strip of steel into a tube and then welding it together (electrically) at high temperature. Better bikes use a seamless tubing which is even in bore throughout. The best bikes use special, cold-drawn alloy steel seamless double-butted tubing. Double-butted means that while the outside diameter of the tube remains constant, it is thicker on the inside at the ends, where greater strength is needed.

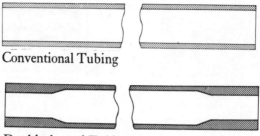

Conventional Tubing

Double-butted Tubing

The method by which the frame parts are attached to each other is important. Bikes with seamed tubing are usually just stuck together and welded, leaving a smooth joint. This is the commonest and weakest type of assembly. The welding, done at high temperatures, robs the metal of strength. High-carbon bike tube steel becomes brittle and subject to fatigue when heated. In better bikes the frame is lugged and brazed, rather than welded. Lugging is the addition of reinforcing metal at stress points, and brazing is done at lower temperatures than welding. Make sure that the job has been done cleanly and neatly on any prospective bike you examine.

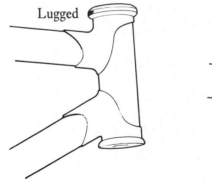

Lugged

Smooth

The very, very best frames are Reynolds 531, Columbus, or Falk, double-butted, with Reynolds generally considered the finest. Reynolds 531 comes in several grades. Read the label to see what you are getting:

Only the top tube, seat tube, and down tube are Reynolds 531 plain gauge tubing.

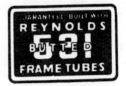

All the tubing is Reynolds 531 plain gauge.

Only the top tube, seat tube, and down tube are Reynolds 531 double butted tubing.

All the tubing is Reynolds 531 double butted.

Chances are you will not be getting double-butted tubing unless you have elected to spend upwards of $300. However, you should at least get seamless lugged tubing, which is used even on low-cost quality bikes. Here are three tests for frame quality. Differences between price ranges should be evident.

(1) Weight. Electric welded tubing and joints are heavy in order to overcome inherent weaknesses of this type of construction and materials.

(2) Lift the bike a couple of inches and bounce it on the wheels. Better frames have more twang and bounce.

(3) Stand to one side of the bike. Hold nearest handlebar with one hand and saddle with the other and tilt bike away from you. Place one foot on end of bottom bracket axle and give a *gentle* push. A good frame will flex and then spring right back. Try

several different bikes to get the feel of it and *be careful,* the idea is to find frames that will give with a gentle push, not bend anything you may encounter. If enough force is applied cheap frames will bend – permanently.

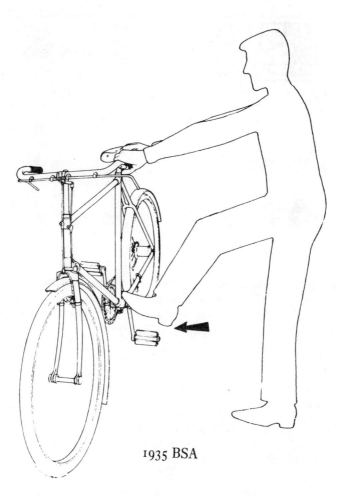

1935 BSA

Bicycle frames come in different designs. The commonest for road and touring use is 72° parallel. This means that the angle to the top tube formed by the seat and head tubes is 72°:

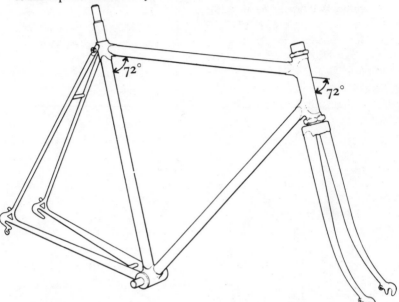

This is the standard design and gives the best combination of road holding, shock absorption, and power transmission. For smooth track work a design such as 74° head and 73° seat is possible. The ride is stiffer, but more power is transmitted to the wheels. A compromise suitable for track and for short distance road work is 73° parallel.

Summary:

One of the most satisfying and important features of a good bike is responsiveness and whip-like flex that you can feel with your whole body. The main determinants of this quality are the frame materials and construction.

In 10-speed bikes, expect the following:

Under $100 – Seamed, smooth-joint frame.

$100 to $250 – Seamless, lugged-joint frame.

Over $250 – Seamless, double-butted, lugged-joint, low-temperature brazed frame.

The brakes

It is the nature of bicycling accidents that the bicyclist more often runs into something than is run into. Good, well-adjusted brakes are vital, and especially in traffic.

Pedal-operated coaster brakes are only for small children who lack the necessary strength to actuate hand levers. Although they are easy to apply, they are hard to control and can lock a wheel, causing a skid. They do not have actual stopping power. It's a skid or next to nothing. Skidding is a bad way to stop since (a) it takes too long; (b) at high speeds it is excessively exciting; and (c) wear and tear on the tires is very high.

Hand-operated caliper brakes come in two types, center and side-pull. These brakes give more control and hence greater stopping power.

Side-pull caliper brakes are commonly used on less costly bikes. They are somewhat inconsistent in performance, although they will work if kept in constant adjustment. Center-pull brakes are better. Because they pull from the center they work in balance, and are more even, precise, and powerful. They are also more reliable and require less maintenance than side-pull brakes.

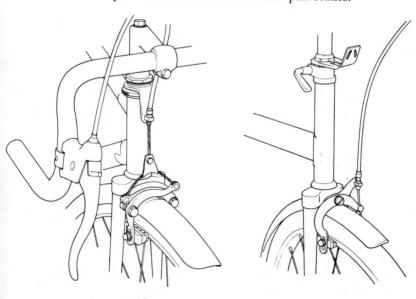

Center-pull   Side-pull

Oddly enough, the most expensive (about $60) brakes available are by Campagnolo and are of the side-pull design. These only work well with a tubular tire rim however, and do not offer any really noticeable improvement over the center-pull design. Weinmann and Universal are two excellent center-pull brands. Mafac brakes have a 3-way adjustment feature at some cost to over-all strength. Badilla is good. Brake adjustments on other brands sometimes involve rather crude alterations in the shape of the yoke.

Summary: Under $100 – Pedal-operated coaster or hand-operated side-pull caliper.

Over $100 – Hand-operated center-pull caliper.

Rims, tires, and hubs

There are two types of rims, those for use with wire-on or "clincher" tires, and those for sew-up or tubular tires. Clincher tires are the best choice for all-round urban use, as they are heavier, more durable, and easiest to repair.

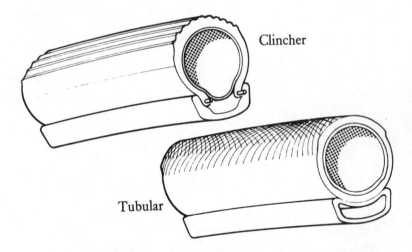

Clincher

Tubular

Tubular tires are lighter and offer less rolling resistance. They are common on high quality bikes. They also cost more and get punctures more easily. Because the tube is sewn into the tire it is impractical to repair on the road, necessitating the carrying of whole spare tires (at $7 to $10 each) which must be glued on to the rim.

While this process is quickly accomplished, it is a drag to lug a spare tire with you wherever you go, since the spare can't be left on the bike when parked on the street. Clincher tires, available everywhere, are the only sensible choice.

Unless you are a speed freak or very seriously into bikes. It is somewhat inconsistent to equip a Reynolds 531 double-butted frame fitted with ultra-light running gear with clincher tires. On the other hand you will go crazy fixing punctures from city riding. One solution favored by freaks is to have two sets of wheels, clinchers for city and regular use, tubulars for tours and races. A good idea if you can afford it. Otherwise, unless the bulk of your riding is on clean country roads and you can always carry a spare, use clinchers.

Rims are either of aluminum alloy or steel. Less costly bikes feature steel rims, which are the most durable and the heaviest. Better bikes feature aluminum alloy rims which are lighter but of course more fragile. Really brutal riding over bumpy terrain may require steel rims but I have found the alloy wheels entirely satisfactory. Better aluminum alloy rims are knurled to increase braking power. This is where the rim has a pattern cut or stamped into the side where the brake shoes touch:

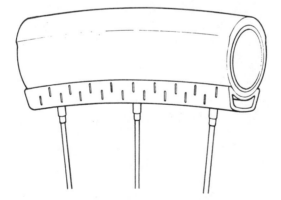

You can of course knurl your own rims with a file, but buy this feature as original equipment if you can. It doesn't cost much extra.

Hubs also come in steel or aluminum alloy. They may use conventional bolts, requiring the use of a wrench to remove the wheel, or quick-release levers which work instantly. This is a desirable feature for bikes that will be stored in the closet, transported by automobile often, or left locked on the street. You can also get lever-type nuts for about $.50 each which are not as fast as the quick-release levers but at least don't require a wrench.

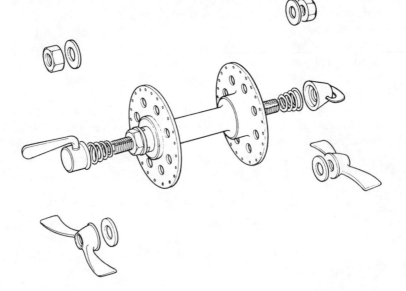

Summary:	Under $100	– Steel rims and bolt on hubs, clincher tires.
	100 to $250	– Alloy rims and quick-release hubs, clincher tires.
	Over $250	– Alloy rims and quick-release hubs, choice of clincher or tubular tires.

Gear changing mechanisms, cranks and chainwheel, and pedals

Nearly all 3-speed bikes use Sturmy-Archer or Shimano multi-speed hubs, no matter what price range. At the core of the design of the 10-speed bike are the derailleurs, which shift the chain from sprocket to sprocket. Differences between brands are to be found in weight, smoothness and precision of shifting, and durability. However, each manufacturer offers several different grades of derailleurs in two different categories, competition and touring. For example, the Campagnolo 'Nuevo Record' (competition) and 'Gran Turismo' are top of the line products of irreproachable beauty and performance, as well they might be with respective price tags of about $40 and $26. Campagnolo's 'Vallentino' economy model on the other hand, has not been well received, and there are plenty of other inexpensive units which are better.

Simplex is a popular brand, although a small but absolutely vital part of the main body on a brand new one I had spontaneously disintegrated, requiring replacement of the entire unit. My experience was not unique, for due to a heavy use of delrin, a plastic, the Simplex is noted for lightness, smooth shifting, a certain degree of fragility, and rapid wear. The most common derailleur is the Huret Allvit. It is made of sturdy metal parts which unfortunately don't always go together properly. Bolts also tend to strip easily. The works are dense and tend to gum up with dirt and oil. But if you can get one that emerged from the factory the way it was supposed to, keep it clean, and don't strip any bolts, it will last a long time. A much better Huret is the 'Svelto' which is light, smooth, and has a wide gear range. The mounting bracket is weak however, and this model might not be the best choice for extended tours.

Not easily available yet in this country is the Maeda 'Sun Tour GT,' a Japanese derailleur of excellent design and quality, and a real value for the money. Shimano is another Japanese manufacturer which produces several different derailleurs. Their 'Lark' and 'Eagle' models, common on low-cost bikes, are good, reliable units at a low cost but are heavy. Their 'Crane GS' is fully competitive in performance and design with the best European units, and is also an excellent buy.

Gearing is a major factor to consider in the choice of derailleurs, and this subject is covered under Fitting. Read this chapter before purchasing a bike.

Cranks and chainwheel. As always, Campagnolo is the finest. Stronglight, T.A., Zeus, and Williams are also good brands. The very finest bikes use cotterless cranks and chainwheels of dural, an aluminum alloy. Medium and low-cost quality bikes use a cottered design of dural, and cheap bikes use cottered steel. A one-piece cranks, chainwheel, and bottom bracket axle design called the Ashtabula is used on many American-made bikes.

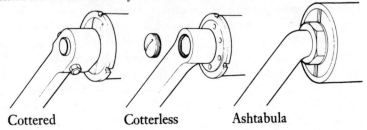

Cottered   Cotterless   Ashtabula

Pedals come in three types: (1) the classic rubber tread; (2) road racing and touring, the design you want; and (3), track racing, which has special teeth for gripping shoes.

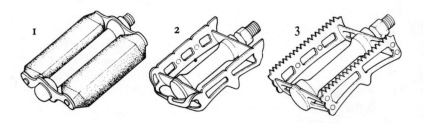

Saddle and handlebars

Three-speed bikes generally have a mattress design wide saddle with coil springs. Racing bike saddles are long and narrow to minimize friction between the legs. Less expensive ones are of plastic, the best of leather, with Brooks the acknowledged leader. On inexpensive bikes the handlebars are of steel, on better bikes of aluminum alloy. The virtues of down-swept bars as opposed to flat bars are discussed in Fitting.

Summary:

As you move up in price from under $100 to over $250 you find an increasing use of aluminum alloy for all parts of the bicycle, except the frame, which in quality machines is of cold-drawn alloy steel, and increasing sophistication of manufacture, such as lugged and brazed frame joints, double-butted frames, and cotterless cranks.

Under $100 – Seamed, smooth-joint frame; coaster or side-pull caliper brakes; clincher tires; rims, bolt-on hubs, cranks and chainwheels, handlebar and stem of steel.

$100 to $250 – Seamless, lugged-joint frame; center-pull caliper brakes; clincher tires; rims, quick-release hubs, cranks and chainwheels, handlebar and stem of aluminum alloy.

Over $250 – Seamless, double-butted, lugged-joint, low-temperature brazed frame; center-pull caliper brakes; choice of tubular or clincher tires; knurled rims, quick-release hubs, cranks and chainwheels, handlebar and stem of aluminum alloy.

There are many different brands of bicycles, and each manufacturer usually produces several grades of machine. To say "Peugeot" means little, since the bike in question may be the utterly basic AO-8 or the very lovely competition PX-10. Major manufacturers generally offer the following categories:

(1) A basic 10-speed with steel parts throughout.

(2) A low-cost quality 10-speed racer with mostly aluminum alloy parts throughout.

(3) The same bike as (2) but equipped for touring with fenders, chainguard, lights and rack, and sometimes 15-speeds (3 chainwheels instead of 2).

(4) Competition-grade ultra-light racing bikes.

We come now to the matter of price. Due to increases in component costs, shipping costs, and taxes, and dollar devaluation, bicycle prices have risen about 50% to 75% in the last two years. The Peugeot UO-8 which cost me $85.00 two years ago is now quoted variously at $135 to $160. The general opinion among importers and bike shop operators is that the situation is now stable and present price levels will prevail. Incidentally, the price increases also affect American bikes, which are for the most part built up from imported components.

I can't possibly cover and evaluate every available bike and therefore am going to make recommendations by category only, and largely to set standards. The bikes that I list are fair values for the money. Diligent shopping may net you a better buy. Many bike shops have one or two specials where you may compromise on color or some other vital consideration for a good break in price or more machine for the money. In any case apply and use the technical information I have given you. There are many many fine bicycles which are not listed here and you will be doing yourself a disservice if you pass them by.

Three-speed bicycles

Standard: Dunelt CM-26 (CL-26 for ladies). Equipped with Sturmy-Archer gears, brazed frame with cutaway lugs, side-pull caliper brakes, fenders and conventional handlebars. A consistently reliable and reasonably-priced bike.

Deluxe: Raleigh "Superbe". Equipped with Sturmy-Archer gears, brazed frame with cutaway lugs, side-pull caliper brakes, lock fork with keys, built-in generator, headlight, and handlebars. A superior bicycle at a higher price than the Dunelt CM-26.

Five- and nine-speed bicycles

These are tourist-type bicycles fitted either with a 5-speed derailleur operated gear, or with a 3-speed derailleur operated gear in conjunction with a 3-speed hub, which gives 9 speeds. I don't see the point of these bikes at all. A regular 10-speed can be purchased with conventional handlebars and soft saddle, if you so desire, and it will out-perform any 5- or 9-speed. Why settle for half a loaf?

Ten- and fifteen-speed bicycles

A word for females: chauvinism is evident in the world of 10-speed bicycles. There are only a few ladies' 10-speed bicycles available and they are structully weaker, frame sizes are more limited, and resale value is lower. My best recommendation is the Peugeot Mixte UO-18, which has the same equipment (and price) as the Peugeot UO-8 described below, except that it comes with a molded leather saddle (instead of racing), upright touring handlebars (downswept bars about $10 extra), frame size is 20″ adjustable, by raising the seat, to 24″, and in blue, white, or emerald green. Another machine is the Gitane Ladies Gran Sport Luxe, with Huret or Simplex derailleurs, mountain gears, Mafac brakes, 20½″ and 22″

frames, conventional handlebars and saddle, and in blue, white, or yellow. The choice is of course yours, but I recommend buying a regular men's bike and simply hiking up long skirts when necessary. You shouldn't be penalized with inferior equipment for the same cash outlay as your male "peers."

Men's 10-speed bikes. If you have less than $100 to spend I recommend the purchase of a used machine. This way you can get the fundamental quality in a machine which makes for really enjoyable bicycling.

Good quality low-cost bicycles

(1) Peugeot UO-8 Trophee de France. Frame of seamless lightweight tubing, special lugs, chrome fork tips and head, in 21″, 23″, 24″, and 25″. Simplex Prestige 637 derailleurs. Chainwheel 10-speed 36 x 52 teeth mountain gear or optional 15-speed 36 x 46 x 52. Atom freewheel 14, 16, 19, 23, 28. Nervar dural 3 pin cranks. Normandy dural high flange hubs with Simplex quick-release axles. Rigida rims with butted rustless spokes. Mafac racer center-pull caliper brakes with covered levers. Michelin 27 x 1¼ gum wall tires. Lyotard No. 36 rattrap pedals. Ava alloy stem and Maes pattern handlebar, white tape covered. Black butt leather racing saddle. Dural racing pump, Mafac toolbag and tools. Blue, white, red, and

emerald green. 27 pounds, complete.

(2) Louison Bobet "Sports". Frame of seamless lightweight steel, lugged and brazed, chrome fork tips, in $20\frac{1}{2}''$, $21\frac{5}{8}''$, $22\frac{7}{8}''$, $24''$, and $25''$. Huret Allvit derailleurs. Chainwheel 15-speed wide range. Cyclo freewheel. Three-pin chrome steel cranks. Dural wide flange quick-release axles. Steel rims, Hutchinson 27 x $1\frac{1}{4}$ tires. C. L. B. dural center-pull caliper brakes with rubber hooded levers. Rattle-trap Tourist pedals with toe clips and straps. Butt leather road-racing type saddle. Dural Sport drop bar with dural stem. Pump, tool bag, tire irons, aluminum fenders, 29 pounds, complete.

Good quality medium-cost bicycles

(1) Louison Bobet C-34. Frame of Reynolds seamless 531, lugged, low-temperature brazed, in $20\frac{1}{2}''$, $21\frac{5}{8}''$, $22\frac{7}{8}''$, $24''$, $24\frac{3}{4}''$, and $25\frac{1}{2}''$. Campagnolo Gran Sport derailleurs. Chrome steel chainwheel. Competition grade freewheel. Stronglight 3-pin cranks. Normandy quick-release highflange alloy hubs. Mavic dural tubular "Sports" rims. Mafac center-pull dural brakes with hooded levers. Lyotard pedals with toe clips and straps. Ideale 41 road-racing butt leather saddle. Robergal stainless spokes. Dural pump. 24 pounds, complete.

(2) Raleigh DL-100. Frame of Reynolds seamless 531 with Capella lugs, in $21\frac{1}{2}''$ and $23\frac{1}{2}''$. Cottered cranks. Williams or Metaur chainwheel. Simplex Prestige 637 derailleurs. Normandy quick-release high-flange alloy hubs. Weinmann or Dunlop dural rims with double-butted spokes. Alloy handlebar and stem. Weinmann or G.B. Synchron center-pull caliper brakes, hooded levers. Brooks B-15 saddle. Toe clips and straps. Alloy half-fenders, plastic chainguard. 26 pounds.

Good quality high-cost bicycles

(1) Peugeot PX-10E Professional Competition Racer. Frame of Reynolds 531 double butted tubing throughout in $72°$ design, Nervex lugs, Simplex ends, chromed fork tips, crown, and rear stays, in $21''$, $23''$ $24''$, or $25''$. Stronglight competition headset. Simplex Prestige 537 Luxe derailleur. Stronglight number 93 dural cotterless crankset. Chainwheel 45 x 52, Atom competition free-wheel 14, 16, 19 20, 23. Sedis chain. Normandy Luxe Competition alloy hubs with Simplex quick-release skewers. Mavic Montlhery

Bicycle made by T. & H. King, blacksmiths,
Wimborne, Dorset, 1872

rims and Hutchinson 9.3 ounce tubular tires. Mafac Racer center-pull brakes. Ava dural handlebars and stem. Lyotard number 45CA dural pedals, with Christophe toe clips and Lapsize straps. Brooks Professional saddle and Simplex seat post. Dural AD-HOC pump, Mafac toolbag and tools. Blue or White. 21 pounds, complete.

(2) Schwinn Paramount P-13. Frame of Reynolds 531 double butted tubing, Nervex lugs, Campagnolo Gran-Sport rear drop-out, Reynolds fork blades with Nervex Pro Crown and Campagnolo Gran Sport fork tips, in 20″, 21″, 22″, 23″, 24″, and 25″. Campagnolo Record derailleurs and cranks. Campagnolo chainwheel 49 x 52, Regina freewheel 14, 16, 19, 21, 24. Campagnolo Record quick-release hubs, Weinmann alloy rims, Dunlop clincher tires. Weinmann Vanquer 999 center-pull brakes. Campagnolo Gran Sport pedals with toe clips and straps. Aluminum alloy handlebars, steel stem. Brooks Professional saddle with Campagnolo seat post. 25¾ pounds, complete. Custom-sized frame, handlebar controls, and tubular tires optional extras.

Children's Bicycles

One attitude towards buying clothes, toys, and other materials for children is something like, "Well, the kid'll grow out of it soon, so let's not waste money. Just get him/her something good enough." Another ploy is, "Well, let's first see if she/he is really interested – then we'll get him/her something better." The victim of this faulty reasoning is the helpless child, who is saddled with some worthless or even painful piece of junk and who is expected to be grateful for it. Cheap bikes for children run from $35 to $40, and good ones from $40 to $50, so the price difference is at most $15. The cheap bike is difficult and unpleasant to ride, and shoddy workmanship and materials guarantee that it will grace the junkpile within a year. Result: total financial loss and total lack of stimulation for the child. The better bike is not only a pleasure to ride, thus insuring your child's fun and interest, but will also survive for a number of years through the hands of several children. It can be passed down in the family or sold for at least half the purchase price. Result: happier *children*, and less net expenditure. If you would like to save money or are on a tight budget, put up 3 x 5 cards advertising for what you want at laundromats, PTA meetings, etc., and get a used bike for $15 to $25.

Incidentally, the use of training wheels will only make learning to ride more prolonged and difficult for your child. He has to learn how to balance, and training wheels only postpone and make harder the inevitable. The best way to teach anybody, young or old, to ride is to let them do it themselves. Lower the seat so that they can comfortably touch the ground with their feet when mounted. All they need to do is push themselves along with their feet, like scootering. Balance and steering ability will come quickly.

Children are ready for their first two-wheel bicycle at about the age of 5, depending on the development and co-ordination of the individual child. The first bike for a child aged 5 to 7 should be a small-frame 20″ wheel featuring:

◎ Pneumatic tires for a comfortable ride, easier pedaling, and effective braking. Solid rubber tires are three times harder to pedal, provide a jolting ride, and give bad braking.

◎ A coaster brake. Caliper brakes cannot be managed by small hands.

◎ Steel steering head bearings. The plastic sleeve bearings used on cheap bikes result in bad handling and steering characteristics, and wear out quickly, compounding the problem.

◎ A sturdy frame with at least two permanent members welded to the steering head. Anything less won't take the punishment kids dish out.

◉ A large seat range adjustment so the bike can grow with the child.

Good, sturdy bikes with all of these features in a price range from $40 to $50 are:

(1) Schwinn J357 Bantam
(2) Vista M901 Speedy
(3) Ross 13613 Deluxe
(4) Columbia 9051 Deluxe Convertible

Any of these bikes may be converted to a girl's model by removing a bolt-on frame member.

For children between the ages of 7 and 9, a 24″ wheel coaster brake bicycle such as the Schwinn 'Fleet' is good. Athletic 8-year-olds and children between 9 and 12 should have a small frame 26″ wheel bicycle with caliper brakes front and rear, and a 3-speed trigger control hub, such as the Schwinn L12-6 'Typhoon'. Be sure your child has a strong enough hand grip before switching to caliper brakes. Children over the age of 12 can use adult bikes.

A popular item with children today is the hi-riser, a 20″ or smaller wheel bike with a small frame and wheelbase, extra high handlebars, banana seat, an excess of flashy hardware, such as car-type gear shift levers, and dramatic names such as Chopper, Jet Star, Dragger, Red Line, and the like. A kind of garbagy distillation of raccoon-tail U.S. of A. consumerism, these bikes come in an astounding assortment of styles, colors, and equipment variations. The high handlebars, short wheelbase, and small wheels make the bikes highly manuverable at low speeds, but otherwise unsafe and difficult to control. For any kind of serious cycling they are not only strictly from hunger, but a real danger and menace to the rider. Hi-risers are suitable only for off the road use and hanging out at the local pizza parlor. I give these machines an especially bad recommendation, do not consider them as bicycles, and consider their purchase for anybody highly irresponsible.

Other Bicycles

Commuting or folding bikes

These are mini-bikes with tiny 16″ or 20″ wheels and hinged, folding frames. Their virtues are (1) easy storage, (2) good luggage capacity, and (3) easy manuverability in tight spots. Their draw-backs are (1) high price, with a cheap, single gear, coaster brake version at $50 to $60, and a 3-speed caliper brake model at $80 to $90, (2) a weight of 40 to 50 pounds which makes them heavy to carry and hard to pedal, (3) an unstable ride due to the small wheels so that oil slicks, manhole covers, and gravel patches are likely to throw you, and (4) poor brakes, even in the caliper versions. This last is critical, since the net effect of the mini-bike's design is to restrict it to short local trips in urban areas. The brakes are totally inadequate for this sort of use and I therefore don't recommend these machines at all. Like hi-risers, which they closely resemble, they are an unsafe liability rather than an asset.

Tandem bikes

All of my experience with tandems has convinced me that these machines require considerably more effort than individually-operated bikes. In addition, they are awkward and therefore danger-ous in traffic. Two riders of unequal strength tend to experience difficulties, with the stronger rider carrying the weaker. Two equally strong riders however, can move a tandem along at a brisk pace, since the over-all bicycle weight is less and wind resistance is cut in half.

INVINCIBLE TANDEM.

This matching of strength and rhythm is rare enough so that the only practical consideration for or against a tandem is togetherness, and the value to be placed on this factor is entirely up to you. If you do opt for a tandem, get a lightweight (40 to 45 pounds) 10-speed and not a balloon heavyweight (90 pounds). Expect to spend about $200 to $250, as for the Gitane Tandem Sport, and be sure to get center-pull caliper brakes.

Adult tricycles

These are popular items in retirement areas and cities in Florida and California. But don't think old age automatically puts you back in the kiddie category. The last time I was in San Francisco I read in the paper that officialdom would not let a bicyclist cross the Golden Gate Bridge (they will now). The bicyclist was especially disappointed because he had just ridden across the U.S. of A. on a racing bike in 30 days (about 100 miles per day) by way of celebrating his 80th birthday. There are a number of bicycle clubs whose

members are all over 70 and who use only two-wheel machines. And I've seen plenty of over-70 skiers having a good time on the slopes, substituting skill and grace for strength and verve. If you can do it, stick with 2-wheelers.

On the other hand don't get suckered into the Great American Youth Cult. There is *always* some possibility of falling off a 2-wheeler, and if you have brittle bones, poor balance and co-ordination, or other problems, you should seriously consider a tricycle.

If you live in a flat area and/or are limited in the movement of your legs, get a fixed gear tricycle, where there is no free-wheeling and the pedals turn when the wheels turn. This has the advantage of carrying limited motion legs through dead spots, and the tricycle can be pedaled backwards. Expect to spend between $100 and $125 for such a machine.

For any kind of hilly terrain get a 3-speed freewheel with low gearing. Expect to spend about $150. Both 3-speed freewheel and single-speed fixed gear tricycles are available from Cyclo-Pedia, 311 N. Mitchell, Cadillac, Michigan, 49601, and Sears, Roebuck. Cyclo-Pedia also has a conversion kit for making a conventional lightweight into a tricycle from $55 to $75, depending on wheel size.

Unicycles

To my mind the unicycle is a toy in the pogo-stick category. Nothing wrong with it – in fact someday I'm going to get one. Cost is about $40 and Columbia's is well thought of.

3. Buying and Keeping a Bike

New Bikes

The best place to buy a new bicycle is a bike store. You can sometimes save money at a department or discount store, but you are virtually guaranteed disproportionate headaches and problems. In the first place, the quality of merchandise is almost always inferior. Secondly, the sad fact is that not even the finest machines are defect-free when they come from the manufacturer. Department and discount stores do not employ trained bicycle mechanics, and so the bikes they sell are often unassembled, or have been put together by some cretin who has literally done more harm than good. It takes a good bicycle mechanic to assemble a new bike without damaging anything, check all the parts, and iron out the inevitable defects. Even then, problems are not likely to be over. If a department or discount store gives a guarantee—few do—they have no mechanics to take care of in-service problems. And if there is some totally basic defect in a machine you buy, it takes weeks for a refund or replacement.

A bike store will assemble the machine. Although you must check their work carefully, chances are they'll do the job right. If some problem comes up later they are available right away to fix it, and so are replacement parts. You get a guarantee, and sometimes a really good one. And you will want to deal with a bike store anyhow, for servicing, parts, accessories, and advice.

The kind of bike store makes a difference. Try to find one that deals only in bicycles. Many major cities now have at least one such shop (see also pp.40-41). Usually they sell machines with a guarantee on parts and labor good for a year and more. Three-year guarantees are not uncommon. Due to a high volume of sales, prices are usually very competitive with discount stores.

The more local a shop you can deal with, the better. Any bike store must meet certain basic requirements in quality of bikes and in service, but convenience means a lot. A guarantee on a store 50 miles away is useless for anything except a major disaster. If there is a local shop and they don't have what you want, talk it over with them. Perhaps they can order a bike for you. If their "brand" of bike is not the one you had in mind take a good look at what they offer. All other things being equal, as they may well be since many

manufacturers use the same components, the convenience of a local shop is an excellent reason to switch " brand". Just make sure you get a fair value. Ask about servicing and parts. If their guarantee isn't good enough, explain the problem. Don't expect however, that they will be able to offer as good a deal as a high-volume super-powered bike store. What you pay a little extra for is the fact that they are around the corner. Also, perhaps the general feeling and vibes are better.

At any rate, stay away from discount and department stores. I have not regaled you with horror stories about machines purchased from such sources, but they are legion, and cover everything from kids' tricycles to ultra-fancy racers. The tiny bit extra you spend in a bike shop buys an awful lot.

Taking Delivery

Anticipate that any new bike will have something wrong with it. Dealing with a good bike store minimizes this possibility but by no means eliminates it. Last summer when I picked up a new dream machine from one of NYC's finest stores I was too bedazzled to give it anything but the most cursory inspection. But as I accelerated away from the store the rear hub and freewheel exploded in a blizzard of metal flakes and chips. Most problems you are likely to encounter are not apt to be so spectacular, but the point cannot be emphasized too strongly that a thorough inspection of any new bike is necessary. The best way to learn what to look for is to read the Maintenance and Repair sections of this book. Here are the main points to watch:

◉ All nuts and bolts are secure. Every last one.

◉ Wheels should spin easily. When held off ground weight of valve stem should pull wheel around so valve is in six o'clock position. Wheel should be centered in fork arms or chain stays. If wheel can be moved from side to side and there is a clicking sound hub cones are out of adjustment. Check that rim is true by holding a pencil next to it and spinning the wheel. Brace the pencil on a fork arm or chain stay to keep it steady.

◉ Pluck spokes. All should be evenly tight and give the same "twang".

◉ Check quality of lug welds on frame. Sight down frame to check for bends.

◉ Brake blocks should hit rims squarely and not drag when

released.

◎ Gears should work smoothly and with no slippage. Test first with wheels off ground and then on a ride.

◎ Pedals and chainwheel should spin easily but without side-to-side play.

◎ Ride the bike around the vicinity of the store for a few miles. You may think that all this is a lot of trouble to go through. I have bought a fair number of new bikes for myself, family, or friends. There was something wrong with every one of them, and a few I rejected outright. You will save yourself a lot of grief if you invest some time at the outset on a careful inspection.

You may be far from a suitable bike store. Here are some that sell bikes and parts by mail:

Wheel Goods
2737 Hennepin Ave.,
Minneapolis, Minnesota, 55408
Catalog $2.

Cyclo-Pedia
311 N. Mitchell
Cadillac, Michigan, 49601
Catalog $1.

Big Wheel Ltd.
Dept K
310 Holly Street
Denver, Colorado 80220
Catalog $2.

Stuyvesant Distributors
10 East 13th St.
New York, N.Y. 10003
Catalog $.75

Just to help out (these lists are very incomplete) here are some of the better-known bike stores, and probably some do business by mail:

Pleasant Valley Shop
P.O. Box 293
Livingston, New Jersey 07039

Cupertino Bike Shop
10080 Randy Lane
Cupertino, California 95014

Turin Bicycle Co-op
2112 North Clark St.,
Chicago, Illinois 60614

Hans Ohrt Lightweight Bikes
9544 Santa Monica Blvd.,
Beverly Hills, California 90210

Thomas Avenia
131 East 119th St.,
New York, New York 10035

Velo-Sport Cyclery
1650 Grove Street
Berkeley, California

Thomas Avenia
10205 Rio Hondo Parkway
El Monte, California

John's Custom Bike Center
741 East Dixie Drive
West Carrolton, Ohio

Gene's
300 East 77th St.
New York, New York 10021

Used Bikes

Good used bikes are elusive, especially when you actually want one. But they are a good way to save money. Expect to pay about 75% of list price for a machine in excellent as-new condition, and about 50% of list for one in average condition.

Sources of used bikes depend on where you live. A few bike stores sell used machines. Most cities and counties have local classified publications listing all kinds of stuff – including bikes – for sale. Check also the classified ads in the regular papers. Sometimes families and people moving sell off furniture and household goods and this often includes a bicycle. Auctions are sometimes good. A good bet in the spring are local bulletin boards at universities and colleges. Put up some cards yourself or take an ad in the student newspaper. Naturally, the more prosaic a bike you seek, the faster you will be likely to find it. But if you just put the word out wherever you go something will turn up – eventually.

When buying a used machine you have to be particularly careful to avoid getting a lemon. Try to find out the history of the machine. It's best if you can talk to the owner. What does his attitude seem to be? Do you think he was interested in his bike and took care of it, or just left it out in the rain? Where did he ride it?

In inspecting the bike, cover all the points listed for a new bike. Pay particular attention to the frame. A certain number of nicks and scrapes are inevitable, but there should be no major dents or rust spots. Be suspicious of new paint.

It will be to your advantage to read carefully through the sections on Maintenance and Repair in this book. Often a used machine will need some work, or some component is not the one you need. You should know the cost and what is involved in replacing or repairing various parts. A $75 racer that needs $75 worth of work is no bargain. On the other hand, if you are looking for a touring bike and find a machine set up with close-ratio competition gears, it costs only about $5 to get a new wide-range gear freewheel.

A final word about used bikes related to the next problem, keeping your bike. There are plenty of stolen bikes for sale. Newspapers publish articles about marketplaces for stolen machines, and in some areas you can even order the type of bike you want. Price is usually about 25% of list, often less. With such a flourishing industry it hardly seems a crime to get a bike this way. It is. Legally and morally. Simply put, you are helping to steal. Additionally, it is not some giant dollar-hungry corporation's candy bar or rip-off piece of junk which you are stealing, but a possession somebody quite probably loves and cherishes.

Carriage propelled by dogs, from France

Keeping Your Bike

The figures on stolen bikes are impressive. As near as I can figure out, about 20% of the bikes in use at any given moment will be ripped off within a year. This is an accurate reflection of the barbaric and primitive savagery of life and people in the U.S. of A. There is nothing like this problem in most other major civilized countries. In England, Holland, and France, for example, many bikes are left on the street unlocked. If you can imagine such a thing, few people would even think to steal them. Here, by way of contrast, theft is so common that the police don't even notice it. One day I came out of school to find a gang of urchins swarming over my bike. They had a five foot long steel bar filched from a construction project with which they were busily trying to break the chain. I noticed with some amusement that not only were passers-by oblivious to the drama, but so were two of New York's finest in a patrol car directly across the street and less than 30 feet away. I told the kids to beat it.

The point is, you are bucking a stacked deck and can expect little help. You have to rely almost entirely on out-thinking the opposition, and on the strength of your locking system. Unfortunately there is no such thing as a fool-proof system. The neatly clipped ends of a $25 "burglar proof" padlock and chain combination which I got from a fancy bike store grace nothing but the garbage heap—I don't care to be reminded of the loss of a really nice machine.

When locking your bike on the street you must:

◎ Use a *case-hardened* chain and padlock. If your bike store does not carry case-hardened chain, find a chain store in the yellow pages. Expect to pay about $20-$25. You have no alternative. A convenient way to carry the chain is encased in an old tire tube and wrapped around the seat post with the padlock clipped to the back of the saddle.

◎ Lock your bike to seriously immovable objects like lampposts, parking signs, heavy fences, etc.

◎ Run the chain through the frame and back wheel. Take the front wheel away with you if you can, or run the chain through it too.

◎ Be very selective about where and when you lock the bike. Slum neighborhoods are a bad bet at any time. Even if the bike itself is not ripped off, kids will often strip away the seat, handlebars, brakes, etc. Business and industrial districts are OK during the day. Always try to pick a busy, well-illuminated spot.

◎ Try to enlist help. The cashier for a movie theatre will usually keep an eye on your bike. Newsdealers and other merchants will often help, and particularly if you do business with them.

Successfully locking your bike is only one part of the problem. Depending on your age, sex, and the value of your bike, you are also subject to direct assault while riding. Usually this crime occurs in parks and other semi-isolated places, and to a lesser extent on slum streets. In form it can vary from seemingly friendly and casual interest on the part of strangers who would like to "try your bike out," to people leaping out of the bushes, knocking you flat, and riding away on your bike. Once assaulted, there is little you can – or should – do unless you are an action freak or have some experience in physical combat. No bike is worth a cracked skull or a knife in the gut. You would not have been jumped in the first place if your opponents did not have an advantage.

The only sensible course is to avoid a confrontation in the first place. Stay out of isolated areas in parks at any time, and stay out of parks altogether at night. If you travel through slum areas move along at a smart pace, and try to stick to well-lit streets. Stay out of lonely business and shipping districts at night. Above all else, be alert. Look for likely ambushes and for people who seem to be unduly interested in you. Keep moving in areas you think are dangerous. You can do 30 mph and easily outrace people on foot.

I won't say that you shouldn't let these problems discourage you from owning a bike. You have to make a realistic evaluation of your own situation. If you work in a crummy neighborhood and your employer won't let you bring your bike inside you're screwed (and should get another job). If you are a woman in a major metropolitan area you are a more likely victim of direct assault. I think that the advantages of owning a bike outweigh the disadvantages. But it would be unfair not to tell you about the problems you may encounter.

If you do get a bike you must accept the possibility that it will be stolen. I succeeded in keeping one bike for years and years. It went when my apartment was ripped off. It can hurt a lot when a cherished and loved bike that you have shared all kinds of experiences with suddenly vanishes to feed some junkie's habit. Try not to forget that it can happen to you, accept it, and the elaborate security precautions you must take will have a slightly less paranoid tone.

A final word about attitude: I used to forgive thieves on the grounds that they were poor. Now that I have seen plenty of places where poor people do not steal this idea is invalid. Still, if you catch somebody trying to steal a bike I think the best thing to do is just tell them to split. Punitive measures, if you are capable of them, will accomplish little, as will moralizing or sermonizing. Calling the police or authorities will only result in teaching the thief how better to steal. The most practical thing would be simply to shoot such people, but this is noisy, messy, and of course illegal. Anyway, the drift of what I am saying is to not blow your cool. You'll only become frustrated. If you don't like this state of affairs, and it is abhorrent to any civilized, sensitive human being, then LOVE AMERICA OR LEAVE IT. Or change it.

4. Fitting

Getting the most out of your bike requires careful fitting, e.g. placement of handlebars, seat, and controls. The standard formulas for this process are the result of considerable work and study by genuine experts and will probably work the best. After you have finished setting your bike up "according to the book" the resulting position may feel a bit odd. Give yourself at least 50 miles to get used to the new arrangement before making alterations. You may find the "odd" position considerably more efficient and less fatiguing than a "comfortable" position. At the same time, no two people are exactly alike, and some variation from the norm may be in order. Just give the orthodox position a fair trial, and make alterations gradually.

For how to make alterations in the position of seat, handlebars, stem, and brake levers, look up Adjustment under the relevant heading in the Maintenance and Repair sections.

Frame

Frame size is measured from the seat lug to the center of the bottom bracket. There are two methods of calculating the proper size:

Inside length of leg from crotch bone to floor, measured in stocking feet, less 9", and

Height divided by 3.

Thus, a person with a 32" inside leg measurement should have a 23" frame, and somebody 6' tall would get a 24" frame. Be sure in any event that you can straddle the frame comfortably with your feet flat on the ground. An under-sized frame can be compensated for to some degree through the use of an extra-long seat post and stem, but an over-sized frame will inevitably slam you in the crotch.

Almost all frames are a 72° parallel design (see p. 20 for what this means) and this is the best set-up for road work. Track and sprint frames sometimes use a steeper seat tube angle of 73° or 74° to get the rider farther forward. This gives greater power for brief bursts, but the ride is harsher. Over the long haul a 72° parallel design works the best.

Saddle

The position of the saddle determines the fitting of the rest of the bike. For most riders the correct fore-to-aft position is with the nose of the saddle $1\frac{3}{4}''$ to $2\frac{1}{2}''$ behind a vertical line through the crank hanger:

Sprint riders and traffic jammers who use brief bursts of sharp energy often use a more forward saddle position. This is the reason sprint frames come with a steeper seat tube angle. For around town use, if you are a vigorous rider, you may like a more forward saddle position. For extended going and best over-all efficiency however, stick within $1\frac{3}{4}''$ to $2\frac{1}{2}''$.

Most saddles are set too low. A rough rule of thumb is that while sitting on the bike with your heel on the pedal at its lowest point, your leg should be straight. This means that when riding with the ball of your foot on the pedal, your leg is almost but not quite fully extended at the bottom of the stroke.

A precise formula for the best saddle height has been worked out in a series of scientific tests. Measure inside length of leg from crotch bone to floor without shoes. Multiply this length (in inches) by 1.09. Example: $32'' \times 1.09$ equals 34.88, or $34\frac{7}{8}''$. Set saddle so distance A from top of saddle to center of pedal spindle in down position with crank parallel to seat tube is $34\frac{7}{8}''$.

This formula has been put together by experts. They found that an alteration in saddle height of 4% of inside leg measurement from the 1.09 setting affected power output by approximately 5%. So once the saddle is set, give it a good long trial before making changes.

Handlebars

Let's settle one thing now: there are many reasons why dropped bars are more efficient and comfortable than flat bars. Here are a few:

(1) A much greater variety of positions is possible. Not only can you select the best position for conditions — like low down when headed into the wind — but being able to shift about and bring different groups of muscles into play greatly increases comfort, to say nothing of power.

(2) Because weight is supported by both the hands and seat, road shocks and bumps rock the body rather than jar it. With conventional flat bars the whole weight of the body rests on the saddle. With dropped bars, not only is weight supported by the arms, but because the body is forward, it tends to pivot at the hips going over bumps. As it happens this is also very desirable from an anatomical point of view: leaning forward stretches the spine, allowing the absorption of shocks, and increases breathing capacity. Conventional bars force the rider into a stiff-spined position where the individual vertebrae of the spine are pinched together. Further, because there is no pivoting give at the hips, each and every jolt and bump is transmitted directly up the spine, greatly increasing fatigue.

(3) The better distribution of weight allowed by dropped bars provides improved stability and steering characteristics.

Positioning of the handlebars is crucial. For conventional use they should be set so that the top bar is just level with the nose of the saddle. Sprint bikes have the bars a whole lot lower, and if you do a lot of traffic riding you may want to set yours down a bit. Mine are about $1\frac{1}{2}''$ lower than the saddle. Just remember that if you opt for short-term speed it will be at some cost to over-all efficiency.

The stem should position the bars so that the distance between the nose of the saddle and the rear edge of the center of the handlebars equals the distance from your elbow to your outstretched finger tips. Another way to determine this distance is to sit on the bike in your normal riding position while a friend holds it steady. Without changing position, remove one hand from handlebars and let arm dangle fully relaxed. Now rotate your arm in a large arc without stretching. If, as your hand comes back to the bar, it is ahead or behind of the other hand, the bars need to be moved. Stems come in increments of length, or you can buy an adjustable stem. This costs and weighs more.

The standard rake for the ends of drop bars is 10° from the horizontal:

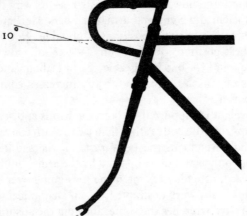

Start with this setting, which makes the tops of the bars level and thus affords the greatest variety of riding positions, and make changes as you desire.

Brakes

Do not tape new bars until you have ridden the bike enough to fully fiddle with and set the position of the brake levers. Most levers are too low. Almost all braking is done from above:

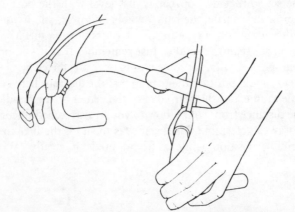

and the levers need to be high enough so that you can stop quickly and without undue effort.

Toe clips

Use them! They virtually double your pedalling efficiency. They may be a little awkward at first, but soon you will be able to slip in and out of them without a thought (see Riding). Be sure to get the size which corresponds to your shoe size. To avoid scratching up fancy shoes, tape the fronts of the clips with a little cloth tape.

Cleats

Cleats are metal strips fastened to the soles of bicycling shoes. Used in conjunction with toe clips they hold your foot to the pedal with a vengeance, and are quite unsafe for traffic riding unless you use very loosely set straps. But they are essential for racing and great for touring. To fit cleats properly ride your bike for a few miles without toe clips so that the soles of your shoes take an impression from the pedals. Then simply position cleats so cleat tunnel is aligned exactly with the pedal marks. Then fit toe clips.

Gearing

Fitting also includes the selection of gearing. Understanding this subject requires some knowledge of basic riding technique. Some of the information I am going to give you now is rather technical. Just use it as you need it.

When I bought my first 10-speed I was surprised to find that the gears, instead of each having a separate range like on a car, overlapped considerably. One gear really wasn't much different than the other. The reason for this is that there is a rate of cadence — the speed with which the cranks are spun around—which is the most efficient. For most people this rate is from 65 to 85 strokes per minute. Racers run 120-130 and up. The idea behind a multitude of gears is to allow the rider to maintain the same cadence regardless of terrain.

In consequence, a racing bike will have close ratio gears, each one much the same as the next, while a touring bike will have wide-ratio gears, with much greater differences between each gear. The reason for this is that touring bikes frequently pack heavy loads up steep grades. They are also — rightly — usually the choice of the novice rider. Only expert riders in good condition can comfortably use close-ratio gears.

What determines ratio? The number of teeth on the front sprocket divided by the number of teeth on the back sprocket. Thus a 60 front and a 15 rear give a 4 to 1 ratio. For competition a typical set-up might be a rear cluster of 23, 21, 19, 17, 15 matched to front sprockets of 49 and 52. For touring it might be 28, 24, 20, 17, 14 rear and 40 to 50 front.

To make everything a little simpler, gear ratios are expressed as a single number. This is the distance in inches one revolution of the cranks will drive a 27″ wheel in a given gear. The formula is:

$$\frac{\text{Number of teeth on front sprocket}}{\text{Number of teeth on back sprocket}} \times \text{wheel diameter} = \text{gear ratio}$$

Here is a chart of the commonly available gears:

Number of teeth on chain wheel

Number of teeth on rear sprocket	24	26	28	30	32	34	36	38	40	42	44	45	46	47	48	49	50	52	53	54	55	56
12	52·1	56·3	60·6	65	69·2	73·8	78	82·4	86·7	91	95·3	97·5	99·7	101·8	104	106·1	108·3	112·7	114·8	117	119·1	121·3
13	48	52	56	60	64·1	68	72	76	80	84	88	90	92	94	96	98	100	104	106	108	110	112
14	44·7	48·2	52	55·7	59·5	63·1	66·8	70·6	74·3	78	81·7	83·5	85·4	87·3	89·1	91	92·9	96·6	98·4	100·3	102·1	104
15	41·6	45	48·5	52	55·6	59	62·4	65·9	69·3	72·8	76·3	78	79·7	81·5	83·2	84·9	86·7	90·1	91·8	93·6	95·3	97
16	39·1	42·2	45·5	48·7	52	55·2	58·5	61·8	65	68·3	71·5	73·1	74·6	76·4	78	79·6	81·3	84·5	86·1	87·7	89·3	91
17	36·7	39·7	42·8	45·8	49	52	55	58·1	61·2	64·2	67·3	68·8	70·4	71·9	73·4	74·9	76·5	79·5	81	82·5	84·1	85·6
18	34·6	37·5	40·5	43·3	46·2	49·2	52	54·9	57·8	60·6	63·6	65	66·4	67·9	69·3	70·7	72·2	75·1	76·5	78	79·4	80·8
19	32·9	35·5	38·3	41	43·8	46·5	49·2	52	54·7	57·5	60·2	61·7	62·9	64·3	65·7	67	68·4	71·2	72·5	73·9	75·2	76·6
20	31·2	33·8	36·4	39	41·6	44·2	46·7	49·4	52	54·6	57·2	58·5	59·8	61·1	62·4	63·7	65	67·6	68·9	70·2	71·5	72·8
21	29·7	32·1	34·6	37·1	39·7	42	44·5	46·1	49·5	52	54·5	55·8	57	58·2	59·4	60·6	61·9	64·4	65·6	66·8	68	69·3
22	28·4	30·7	33	35·4	37·9	40·2	42·5	44·9	47·3	49·6	52	53·1	54·4	55·5	56·7	57·9	59·1	61·5	62·6	63·8	65	66·1
23	27·1	29·3	31·6	33·9	36·2	38·4	40·6	43	45·2	47·5	49·8	50·8	52	53·1	54·3	55·4	56·5	58·8	59·9	61	62·1	63·3
24	26	28·1	30·3	32·5	34·7	36·8	39	41·2	43·3	45·5	47·7	48·6	49·9	50·9	52	53·1	54·2	56·3	57·4	58·5	59·5	60·6
25	25	27	29·1	31·2	33·4	35·4	37·4	39·5	41·6	43·7	45·8	46·9	47·8	48·9	49·9	51	52	54·1	55·1	56·1	57·2	58·2
26	24·1	26	28	30	32·8	34	36	38	40	42	44	45	46	47	48	49	50	52	53	54	55	56
28	22·3	24·1	26	27·8	29·7	31·6	33·4	35·3	37·1	39	40·9	41·8	42·7	43·6	44·6	45·5	46·4	48·3	49·2	50·1	51	52
30	20·8	22·3	24·8	26	27·5	28·6	31·2	32·7	33·8	36·4	37·9	39	39·7	40·5	41·6	42·3	43·1	44·9	45·7	46·8	47·5	48·3

For 26" wheels

Number of teeth on chain wheel

	24	26	28	30	32	34	36	38	40	42	44	45	46	47	48	49	50	52	53	54	55	56
12	54·1	58·5	63	67·5	72	76·5	81·1	85·5	90	94·5	99	101·2	103·5	105·7	108	110·2	112·3	117	119·3	121·5	123·7	126
13	49·8	54	58·1	62·3	66·4	70·6	74·7	78·9	83·1	87·2	91·4	93·4	95·5	97·6	99·7	101·8	103·9	108	110	112·1	114·2	116·3
14	46·2	50·1	54	57·8	61·7	65·5	69·5	73·3	77·1	81	84·9	86·7	88·7	90·6	92·6	94·5	96·4	100·3	102·2	104·1	106	108
15	43·2	46·8	50·4	54	57·6	61·1	64·8	68·4	72	75·6	79·2	80·9	82·8	84·6	86·4	88·2	90	93·6	95·4	97·2	99	100·8
16	40·5	43·7	47·2	50·6	54	57·2	60·9	64·1	67·5	70·9	74·3	76	77·6	79·3	81	82·7	84·4	87·8	89·4	91·1	92·8	94·5
17	38·1	41·2	44·4	47·6	50·8	54	57·2	60·3	63·5	66·7	69·9	71·5	73·1	74·6	76·2	77·8	79·4	82·6	84·1	85·7	87·3	88·9
18	36	39	42	45	48	51	54	57	60	63	66	67·5	69	70·5	72	73·5	75	78	79·5	81	82·5	84
19	34·1	36·8	39·7	42·6	45·5	48·2	51·1	54	56·8	59·7	62·5	64	65·3	66·6	68	69·4	71·1	73·9	75·3	76·7	78·1	79·5
20	32·4	35·1	37·8	40·5	43·2	45·9	48·7	51·3	54	56·7	59·4	60·8	62·1	63·4	64·8	66·2	67·5	70·2	71·5	72·9	74·5	75·6
21	30·8	33·4	36	38·6	41·1	43·7	46·4	48·9	51·4	54	56·6	57·9	59·1	60·4	61·7	63	64·3	66·9	68·1	69·4	70·7	72
22	29·4	31·9	34·3	36·8	39·2	41·6	44·2	46·6	49·1	51·5	54	55·2	56·5	57·6	58·9	60·1	61·4	63·8	65	66·2	67·5	68·7
23	28·1	30·5	32·8	35·2	37·5	39·9	42·4	44·6	47	49·3	51·6	52·8	54	55·2	56·3	57·5	58·7	61	62·2	63·6	64·5	65·7
24	27	29·2	31·5	33·7	36	38·2	40·5	42·8	45	47·3	49·5	50·7	51·8	52·9	54	55·1	56·3	58·5	59·6	60·7	61·8	63
25	25·9	28	30·2	32·4	34·6	36·7	38·9	41	43·2	45·4	47·5	48·6	49·7	50·8	51·8	52·9	54	56·2	57·2	58·3	59·4	60·4
26	24·9	27	29	31·2	33·2	35·3	37·4	39·5	41·5	43·6	45·7	46·7	47·8	48·8	49·9	50·9	51·9	54	55	56	57·1	58·1
28	23·1	25	27	28·9	30·8	32·8	34·8	36·6	38·6	40·5	42·4	43·7	44·4	45·3	46·3	47·2	48·2	50	51·1	52	53	54
30	21·6	23·2	25·1	27	28·6	30·6	32·4	34·2	36	37·5	39·6	40·5	41·4	42·1	43·2	44	45	46·8	47·5	48·6	49·4	50·2

Number of teeth on rear sprocket

In general, 100 is the top range and is hard to push, 90 is more common, and 80 the usual speed gear. 60 and 70 are the most often used, 40 and 50 are for hills. Below 40 is for extremely steep terrain and heavy loads. Most people gear too high and pedal too slowly. This increases fatigue. It is much better to pedal briskly against relatively little resistance.

There are other factors besides range to consider in setting up gears. Ease of transition from one gear to another is important. If you have to shift both front and back sprockets every time it is laborious. For example:

		Rear				
		14	17	21	26	31
Front	52	100	83	67	54	45
	47	90	75	60	49	41

means that to run up through the gears consecutively requires continuous double shifts. On the other hand, a set up like:

		Rear				
		14	15	17	19	21
Front	54	104	97	86	77	70
	38	73	68	60	54	49

means that you can run up through the gears using only one shift of the front derailleur. (Never use the small front to small rear or big front to big rear. I will explain why later.)

If you use wide gaps front and rear there is almost bound to be some duplication of gears:

		Rear				
		14	17	21	26	31
Front	52	100.3	82.6	66.8	54	43.2
	42	81	66.7	54	43.6	35.1

and yet curiously enough, many good bikes are set up this way. It really depends on what you want the bike for, because in balancing the various factors of range, ease of shifting, and number of different gears, you are just going to have to make some compromises. For novice riders I would suggest the following:

Hilly terrain
Competition – 45 x 52 front, 14, 16, 19, 20, 23 rear.
Touring – 36 x 52 front, 14, 16, 19, 23, 28 rear.

Flat terrain
Competition – 49 x 52 front, 15, 17, 19, 21, 23 rear.
Touring – 40 x 54 front, 14, 16, 19, 23, 26 rear.

Compromise
Touring – 40 x 50 front, 14, 17, 20, 24, 28 rear.

I make these recommendations with some misgivings for there is one problem or another with all of them. There always is, but these are stock gearings with which you can do quite a bit. Each person of course has his own personal preferences, and you should work out gearing to suit your own needs. I, for example, don't care a fig about competition, and am mostly interested in traffic jamming and touring. On my all-time favorite bike (lost to a junkie) I had 46 x 60 front and 13 through 30 rear, which got me incredulous and pitying regard from bike-wise friends. It suited me perfectly. The 46 front running through the 30 rear gave me a 41 gear which got me up nearly everything. When in town I used only the 60 front and the three middle gears of the back sprocket, thus minimizing shifting. Down hills and long shallow gradients the super-heavy 60 front and 13 rear drove the bike along like a bomb. In short, it was ultra-wide range gearing also suitable for short sprints.

Such esoteric gearing is not easy to get. I have been trying now for a few years. Most front sprockets stop at 52. A few expensive brands go to 54 or rarely, 56. The 13 rear is according to one source hard on chains. I didn't find this to be true but perhaps this is the reason why they are hard to get. Anyway, you can go a long way with conventional gearing. Since the loss of Golden Flash I've used more or less stock gearing and found it satisfactory.

If you do elect to muck around with gear ratios you will have to take derailleur capacity into account. Besides shifting the chain from sprocket to sprocket, the rear derailleur also keeps the chain taut. A 14 through 30 rear and a 36 x 54 front gives a variation in chain slack (between the 36 to 14 and 54 to 30) which exceeds the capacity of some derailleurs. Derailleur capacity is a function of design: competition units do not have to cover a wide range and can therefore be much lighter; touring units are heavier and sturdier. Generally, capacity is marked on the box as for example 13-24-36-53. The outer figures give the high gear, the inner, the lower. Some advertised figures are as follows:

Brand	Rear Range	Front and Rear
Simplex Prestige	13–28	37
Huret Allvit	13–28	28
Campagnolo Nuevo Record	13–30	32
Campagnolo Gran Turismo	13–36	43
Sun Tour GT	13–34	40

For wide range gearing the Campagnolo Gran Turismo is a whirlaway winner. It is sturdy, beautifully made and designed – and heavy.

You will have to decide for yourself which elements in the weight *vs.* range balance are the most important. Here is the final tidbit to take into account and round out an already confusing picture: you don't need the full range of the derailleur. You should not ever run the big front sprocket to the big rear, or the small front to the small rear, because it causes the chain to cut across at too severe an angle, causing excessive wear, usually rubbing of the derailleur gates, and reduced efficiency.

So . . . the important range is between the large front sprocket to the next to largest back sprocket and the small front sprocket to the next to smallest rear sprocket. Since this is a more limited range with a little diddling you can use a competition derailleur with relatively wide range gears. The advantage is lighter weight and improved performance.

This business of cross-angle strains on the chain bears on the subject of triple front chainwheels. These units are the choice of many experienced tourists for mountain country and packing heavy loads, as they give the most range. Because of cross-over problems however, you do not get that many extra gears. In addition, triple chainwheels are difficult to adjust and align, and the derailleur cages tend to get screwed up. Some manufacturers have simply stopped selling 15-speed bikes. Unless you really need the extra range I'd advise staying away from this combination.

5. Riding

Anybody can ride a bicycle. You just get aboard and pedal. Heh. Try following an experienced tourist on an 100-mile run or a competition rider around the track. Physical condition of course plays a part, but here technique counts more than anything else. Fifty-year-old grandmothers can and do run rings around fit young adults. Attention to the basics of technique will make riding easier and more enjoyable, and give you greater freedom than if you had not bothered with the subject at all.

Of course even basic technique varies somewhat with conditions. And there is a lot more to riding than technique. The following chapters on traffic jamming, and touring and racing, amplify considerably on the information you need in order to cycle safely and comfortably.

Shifting

Take it easy when first learning to shift. Once you get the knack you can make smooth split-second gear changes, but let your skill develop gradually and avoid damaging "clunk" sounding shifts.

3-Speeds: To shift up to a higher gear, ease pressure on pedals, move selector to next gear, resume pressure. Extra-fast shifts may be made by maintaining pedal pressure, moving the selector, and then pausing momentarily when the shift is desired. If done too hard this may damage gears. Going down to 1st from 2nd or 3rd and coming to a stop, back-pedal slightly. If not stopping, use same procedure as for upshifts.

10-Speeds: Never, ever shift a 10-speed unless pedalling. To see why, hang your bike up so that the rear wheel is off the ground, rotate the cranks, and manipulate the gear shift levers so you can see how they work. Shifting a 10-speed without pedalling may result in a bent or broken chain or gear teeth. If you park your bike on the street always give the gears a visual check to make sure passers-by have not fiddled with them. It happens often.

When going up or down through the gears ease pedalling pressure during shift. The shift levers do not have stops for the different gears, and you have to learn where they are by feel. Do not let the derailleur cages rub the chain. Sometimes it is necessary to make a small adjustment in the front derailleur when using a wide range of rear sprockets in order to prevent this. Do not run the big front

sprocket to the big rear sprocket, or the small front to the small rear. It causes the chain to cut across at too severe an angle, greatly increasing wear and reducing efficiency. Proper shifting should also take into account the demands of cadence (see below).

Pedalling

Ride with the ball of your foot on the pedal, not the heel or arch. The fundamental technique for easy cycling is called ankling. This is where the foot pivots at the ankle with each revolution of the crank. Start at the top of the stroke (12 o'clock) with the heel slightly lower than the toes. Push with the ball of the foot and simultaneously pivot at the ankle on the downstroke so that the foot levels out between 2 and 3 o'clock, and continue this motion so that at the bottom of the stroke the toes are lower than the heel:

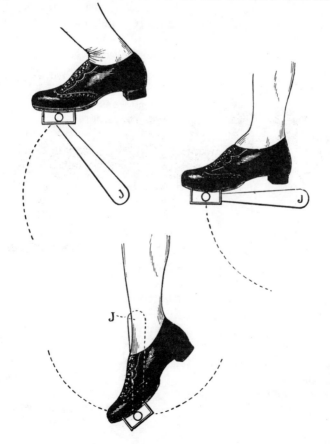

With toe slips pull up on the upstroke as well. The main thing to strive for is smoothness and steady, even pressure. Practice this slowly, in a high gear, and away from traffic so you can concentrate on watching your feet.

Toe clips are a great boon. By allowing you to pull up on the pedals as well as push down they virtually double pedalling efficiency. They are completely safe. Smooth-soled conventional shoes can always be slipped out even when tightly strapped down. If using bicycling shoes and cleats, keep the straps loose in traffic. The technique for setting underway is simple: start with loose straps. Straddle the bike, slip a foot into a pedal at the 1 o'clock position, and tighten the strap. Push off, using the downstroke of this crank to get you underway, and simultaneously reach down with the free foot, give the pedal a light tap to spin the toe clip around to the proper position, slip foot in, bring crank around to 12 o'clock position, and tighten strap. It sounds more complicated than it is. The key is the deft, light tap to the pedal to bring the toe clip around so you can slip your foot in. Practice will soon make it second nature. When coming to a stop reach down and loosen one strap so you can get your foot back in easily when underway again. Do not worry about being trapped by toe clips. I have made zillions of emergency stops and have always been able to get my feet free. On the other hand, do not tempt fate by riding in heavy traffic with ultra-tight straps. And if you use sneakers or other soft-soled shoes (bad — not enough support), or cleated bicycling shoes, keep the straps loose when conditions warrant.

Cadence

This subject was mentioned in connection with gearing. Briefly, human beings pedal most efficiently at a certain number of strokes per minute. The optimum cadence varies with the physical condition and technique of the individual rider. Generally, novices run from 60 to 85 strokes per minute, experienced tourists approach 100, and racers run 120–30 and up.

Most people gear too high and pedal too slowly. They don't think they are getting anywhere or getting any exercise unless they are pushing against resistance. It is precisely this pushing which creates needless fatigue. It is much better to pedal rapidly against relatively little resistance. Especially when first starting with a bike, always try to pedal as rapidly as you can without going into orbit.

Soon you will find your natural cadence, and should always try to maintain this as a uniform rate of pedalling. Allow this to be one of the primary functions of the gears, and always shift up or down as necessary to maintain an even cadence. Learn to shift just before you need the new gear. Do not let a hill slow down your cadence, for example, but shift just before you hit it, and as needed going up. The way you will be able to churn along will be absolutely amazing.

Bumps

When you come to bumps, pot-holes, cables, etc., put most of your weight on the pedals and handlebars. This allows the bike to pivot underneath you, reducing shock for both you and the bike. You know how motorcycle scramble riders stand up on the pegs? Like that.

Braking

Try to use your brakes as little as possible. This will help you to "look ahead" and know what is going to happen in advance. With caliper brakes be careful of braking too hard and skidding. Under slippery conditions or when banked way over for a corner favor the rear brake. Going down long hills avoid overheating the brake shoes by pumping (on-off-on-off-on, etc.) the brakes.

THE AMERICAN STAR MACHINE

6. Traffic Jamming

Every rider must know how to ride on streets and highways shared with motor vehicles, the same way if you walk you have to know how to cross the street. Beyond this, for many people 99% of their riding is in traffic, and they might as well make it as safe and enjoyable as possible. I have the worst misgivings about this chapter, for on the one hand I want you to use a bicycle as much as possible, but there is no way I can tell you that riding in traffic is safe. In plain fact it is dangerous. The other side of the coin is that taking a bath is dangerous too. There are some things one has or wants to do, accepting and attempting to prepare for attendant dangers. Each person needs to make her/his own evaluation of the amount and kind of traffic riding that suits him/her. Although the basic principles are the same, there is a considerable difference between mixing it up with heavy weekday commuter traffic and cycling a few blocks to the park on Sunday.

This chapter contains a multitude of facts and suggestions, but the most important thing I have to tell you about riding under any conditions, *and especially in traffic*, concerns psychological attitude and attentiveness. You must at all times be alert, and know everything that is going on, from the size of the pebbles on the road to the debris which might fall on you from a construction project to the number and type of vehicles before and behind you — absolutely everything. Traffic riding requires total concentration. There is no place for woolgathering here, or idyllic pastoral pleasures. If you don't pay attention, you may die.

To illustrate the point: many people are fond of saying with respect to motor vehicles that "speed kills." Yet a few years ago when the speed limit on a major parkway was reduced the accident rate went up. The slower travelling motorists became bored and paid less attention. Result: more accidents. People on their way to an accident will get there whether they are doing 30 or 70 mph. It is a function of attentiveness more than anything else.

Attentiveness has benefits. First of all, total engagement is refreshing. For example, I like physical challenges but spend most of my time pushing a pencil. For me the change of pace represented by traffic jamming is at times exhilarating. It does, as they say, take your mind off your troubles. Secondly, once you gain a little experience you will hopefully still be alert, but relaxed. Is crossing the street a

C. B. DeMille production for you? In a more relaxed state you will appreciate the benefits of attentiveness, and see more, notice more, feel more. Getting from one place to another will be a distinctly real experience, and something *you* do.

I would like to deal with two other drawbacks to traffic jamming which unfortunately have no redeeming features:

Hyperventilation*

The inhalation of exhust fumes and other pollutants is a serious health hazard. The automobile contributes up to 85% of all air pollution in urban areas. As a cyclist not only are you at nose level with the maximum concentration of the pollution, but you are breathing harder and faster (hyperventilation). Estimating the precise degree of possible or actual damage is difficult. One statistic is that the average urbanite inhales the equivalent in particles and poisons of two packs of cigarettes a day. Does this translate for the bike rider as 4 packs of cigarettes a day? Five? Six?

Cars emit lead, unburnt gas, nitrogen oxides, sulphur oxides, carbon monoxide, and small quantities of grit. The worst for the cyclist are lead and carbon monoxide.

According to Dr. Derek Bryce-Smith, Professor of Chemistry at Reading University, there is a good chance that airborne lead is causing real physical damage to large numbers of children today. He has also suggested that a portion of mental illness may be due to otherwise undetectable brain damage from lead pollution. Lead poisoning has been listed as a cause in the death of zoo animals.

Carbon monoxide is the greatest immediate risk for the cyclist. It is a classic poison which interferes with the oxygen-carrying capacity of the blood. Long before it kills, this action results in decreased alertness, headaches, vague dizziness, and nausea. This dehabilitation adds to the hazard of traffic jamming.

The concentration in the air in many urban areas of both lead and carbon monoxide is already far above recommended levels. These levels are themselves suspect, for in the Soviet Union the permitted concentration of lead is 100 times lower than in the U.S. of A. Considering that the auto industry has now for decades resisted building pollution-free engines for reasons of profit, it is most likely that we have false standards and a tremendous minimizing of the real hazard.

*Thanks to Francis Arnold for much of the information here.

Mental illness, headaches, animal deaths, Soviet standards, two packs a day, and other tidbits of information are not readily translatable into an accurate assessment of damage, and particularly not for the cyclist, who rides through the very worst of the pollution. But the simple fact is that I get sick with headache, eye pains, nausea, and general malaise when I ride on smoggy days, and particularly the days which have a yellowish tint.

I would advise against riding at all on high air pollution count days. Try to stay clear of smoke-factory trucks and buses, and pick roundabout routes that favor parks and less travelled streets. Most gas masks will only filter out grit, but of course the sight of you using one would be wonderful guerilla theatre.

The hazard of air pollution should not be minimized at all: the benefits you gain from the exercise of riding may well be offset by the damage caused by inhaling the chemicals, poisons, and other wondrous substances freely released into the air we breathe.

Females

I am ashamed to write about this, yet it is a reality. Females are subject to harassment from motorists and passersby. This ranges from relatively harmless if insulting lewd comments to outright assault, where a motorist will reach out of his car to knock a moving female cyclist to the pavement. I don't have statistics on this latter sort of thing, but have heard of enough incidents so that there is no question but that it happens, and is something any female cyclist must take into account. Incidentally, if you witness such an assault and can possibly do so, beat the assailant up black and blue. Such people are cowards who can be kept in check only through fear and intimidation. Get license numbers and all that, but the wheels of justice tend to miss these characters. An attack from a car on a defenseless bicyclist merits putting the assailant in a hospital.

There are innumerable physical hazards to keep a lookout for while riding in traffic, but it is motor vehicles which are your main concern. In riding your bike you are something of a pioneer. The U.S. of A. is not really ready for the bicycle. Theory and law say that the bicycle is a vehicle which must be operated according to the rules of the road and which has the same privileges as other vehicles. Fact says otherwise. The American motorist is absolutely convinced that his vehicle gives him the complete right of way.

Anything which obstructs his forward progress — like a slow moving bicycle — just shouldn't be there. He may be wrong, but it is essential for your survival to understand how he thinks. As a cyclist you don't really exist for him. As often as not he will cut you off, make turns in front of you, or sit on your tail honking furiously when there is no room to pass. It never even occurs to him to put on his brakes and give you room to maneuver, as he would for another car.

Riding successfully in traffic requires a blend of determination and knowing when to give in. For example, try never to block overtaking cars. At the same time if it is unsafe for you to let them pass, don't hesitate to take full possession of your lane so that they *can't* pass. Both you and the other human have exactly the same right to use the street or highway. Just because he/she has a motor vehicle confers no additional rights or privileges, and in fact the wasteful consumption of energy and vicious pollution of the environment for which her/his vehicle is responsible is a serious infringement of your rights. It is important that you understand and believe this. You have nothing to apologize for. You are not "blocking" or "in the way." At the same time you have to be practical. You are in a land of primitive savages. A lot of people behind the wheel are authentic maniacs. No matter how right you are, any confrontation with a motor vehicle will wind up with you the loser.

There are enough aspects and tricks to traffic jamming so that I am simply going to run them as a list. Before doing so, a brief discussion about traffic regulations.

The rules of the road, which you are legally required to obey, need to cut both ways. In England for example, cyclists meticulously observe traffic lights, signs, and regulations. Riders signal all turns, stops, and the like. In turn, motorists treat the cyclists as equals. Nobody ever leans on a horn and crawls up somebody's behind if a bicycle leads a pack of cars away from a light. The English are fond of traffic circles which resemble a Dodge-em at Coney Island. It takes a little cool, but you can confidently sail out into the middle of one of these on a bike. Because a cyclist is in fact accorded proper privileges and vehicle status, it is really unthinkable not to obey traffic regulations. In England, even when the coast is clear I always stop for a red light. I desperately want the protection equal status gives me.

In the U.S. of A. no such rules apply. Most books tell you to

abide by the traffic regulations. This often is not practical. More-over, because you can never rely on your "rights" to protect you, you have to engage in a form of defensive riding which assumes that if there is some way for somebody to get you, they will. Accordingly, when the coast is clear rules have little binding effect. You just aren't thinking that way. Remember however, you can get a summons for traffic violations on a bicycle, and if you supply a driver's license as identification (which you are not required to do), any convictions become part of your driving record.

Rolling

◉ Hands near or on brake levers at all times. If you need to stop as quickly as possible and are not going too fast, twist the front wheel as you apply the brakes. The bike will melt into the ground in a controlled crash as the wheel and forks buckle.

◉ Be alert. There is plenty to watch for. Keep your eyes constantly moving. When looking behind don't twist your head, duck it down. Easier to do, quicker, and smoother. Do this constantly. You might have to swerve to avoid an obstacle or serious accident, and must know if you have the room or not.

◉ Be definite. Save meandering for country lanes where you can

see for a long way in both directions. Ride in a straight line. Signal all turns clearly. Make right turns from right lane and left turns from left lane, if on a wide street. If you are going to do something, do it. Being definite takes the form of a certain amount of aggressiveness. Don't get bulldozed into immobility — nobody is going to give you a break. Make and take your own breaks. As far as most other drivers are concerned you either don't exist or are some alien foreign object which they want behind them. Draw attention to yourself and be super-clear about your intentions. Colorful clothing and/or a bright hat are a good idea.

◎ Be defensive. Always assume the worst. You can't see around the stopped bus? *Assume* a pregnant lady who is the sole support of 21 children is going to come prancing out. There is a car waiting to cross your lane? *Assume* it will, because *it will*. In 4 out of 5 accidents involving bicycles and motor vehicles, the motor vehicle committed a traffic violation. Always ride within a margin of control which allows you to stop or escape should absolutely everything go wrong.

◎ Look for openings in traffic, driveways, streets, garages, etc. that you can duck into should the need arise. Try to plan where you would go should you and the bike part company. The natural tendency in a collision situation is to try desperately to stop. Many times your interests will be better served by launching yourself over an obstacle. Far better to hit the pavement at an angle than a car head-on.

◎ While not exceeding a speed which gives you control, try to keep moving. Within reason, avoid using brakes. This will have the effect of making you figure out well in advance what traffic situations are going to occur. There is a car double-parked in the next block. Are you going to be able to swing out? Also, a lot of the danger from other vehicles in traffic comes from differences in velocity. If you are going slow, cars bunch up behind, crowd, become impatient, etc. A racing bike can easily keep up with and pass a lot of traffic. You may find it a bit unnerving to run neck and neck with cabs and trucks at first, but it is safer than offering a stationary target. Try to *integrate* yourself with the traffic.

◎ To this end, always be in a gear low enough to give you power and acceleration. In heavy traffic an even cadence is difficult to maintain, but try to keep your feet churning away and avoid getting stuck in a "dead" high gear. As a cyclist you have only a fraction of the power available to the motorist. To stay integrated with traffic requires that you be prepared to accelerate hard and quickly.

◎ On the other hand, do not tailgate. Car brakes are better than bike brakes. Most bike accidents consist of the bicycle running into something. Leave plenty of room up front. This is where motorists accustomed to running bumper-to-bumper will try to pressure you from behind, even though you are moving at the same speed as the car you are following. Maintain position and if they give you the horn give them the finger.

◎ Be extra-cautious in intersections where you already have right of way. Cars coming from the opposite direction and turning left will frequently cut right across your path. Even if the vehicle is seemingly waiting for you to pass, don't trust it, for at the last moment it will leap forward. Cabs are particularly bad for this. Letting a motor vehicle precede you to clear the way is often a good tactic.

Another danger at intersections is cars coming up alongside from behind and then making a sudden right turn. Cabs love to do this. One way to stop it is for you to be in the center of the lane. However, if the intersection you are entering has a light which is going to change soon, then traffic from behind may be storming up at a breakneck pace. You'd better be out of the way.

◎ In any city anywhere in the world taxicab drivers are your worst hazard. All things are relative, and in London for example, most cabbies are decent. In the U.S. of A. cabbies have the highest ulcer rate of any occupational group, as well they might considering their working conditions and how they drive. Abilities vary, but most are just no good. New York City cabbies are the bottom of the barrel.

The cab driver is your enemy. He is *accustomed* to bulldozing and bluffing his way around by main force. It is second nature, and does not even require hostile intent on his part. It is just something he does. Every day. You, on a 30-pound bicycle just haven't got a chance against his 5000-pound cab. And many cabbies do take a perverse pleasure out of screwing you up. Perhaps they are resentful of anyone having fun on a bike. Who knows. At any rate, if there is anybody who is going to cut in front of you, brake suddenly, etc., it is the cabbie. Cabs are the enemy.

◎ Very often you will be riding next to parked cars. Be especially careful of motorists opening doors in your path. Exhaust smoke and faces in rear-view mirrors are tips. Even if a motorist looks right at you and is seemingly waiting for you to pass, give her/him a wide berth. Believe it or not, you may not register on his/her consciousness, and she/he may open the door in your face.

◎ Keep an eye on the road surface. Watch out for broken glass— endemic to the U.S. of A. — stones, potholes, etc. Plenty of bumps and potholes are big enough to destroy a bike — and you. Going over bumps, cables, etc. get off the saddle and keep your weight on the pedals and handlebars.

Quite a few things can dump a bike:

◎ Oil slicks in the center of traffic lanes at busy intersections and on sharp curves. When cars stop or turn hard a little oil drops off. The resulting slick can send you off the road or sliding out into the middle of a busy intersection.

◎ Newly wet streets. There is a light film of oil which until it is washed away mixes with the water to make a very slippery surface.

◎ Wet manhole covers and steel plates can dump you in a hurry. I have seen this happen often.

◎ Wet cobblestones.

◎ Wet autumn leaves.

◎ Gravel and sand.

◎ Storm sewers. American storm sewers are just the right size to swallow up a bicycle wheel.

◎ Ride with the traffic. Sometimes when there is no traffic coming the other way, it is better to ride in the opposite lane.

◎ The velocity of traffic on free-way style streets which have no parking is usually too high to permit safe cycling. If you run in the center of the lane, you block traffic. If you to go the side, cars whiz by you at high speeds with only inches to spare. Stick to streets with parked cars and look out for opening doors.

◎ Cars and trucks pulling out. They do it unexpectedly and without signaling. Look out for driveways, building entrances, construction projects, cab ranks, and any other possible source of a vehicle. Remember, you don't exist for many drivers. They look right at you, the image is flashed on their brain, but they don't comprehend. They don't *see* you.

And perhaps some do. One time I had the light going into an intersection with a police car waiting on the cross street. The eyes of the driver fixed steadily on me and he waited until I was just going through the intersection before pulling through a red light and right in front of me.

◎ Pedestrians are another unreliable bunch. They don't think 200 pounds of bike and rider coming toward them at 30 mph means anything, and will frequently jaywalk right in your path. Your odds are much better here than when mixing it up with a car, but even so any collision is going to hurt you, the pedestrian, and your bike. Use a horn, yell — and give them the right of way if you have to.

◎ Kids. As much of a hazard to the cyclist as to the motorist. Any child has the potential to suddenly race out into the street.

◎ Other cyclists. I don't know why, but many cyclists and especially children cyclists are erratic. Give them a wide berth.

◎ Yellow glasses are good for city riding to keep the dirt out of your eyes.

◎ Lights are a legal requirement at night. I have learned from bitter experience that they don't make much difference to motorists. There is a French-made white front/red rear flashlight which straps to the arm or leg and therefore gets waved around a lot. It weighs only 5 ounces. See Accessories for a fuller discussion of lights. I like a large, permanently mounted rear reflector. Lights have a habit of failing.

◎ Alcohol and cannabis. In a recent experiment a group of drivers were tested for driving ability. Then half the group was stoked up on booze, the other half stoned out on hash or grass, and driving ability measured again. The booze group became more belligerent and aggressive, for example passing more often, and demonstrated slowed reaction times, while the dope contingent slowed down, became easy going and accommodating, but showed no diminishment of reaction time to emergency situations.

All these endless cautions are depressing. It seems that riding in traffic involves girding yourself for battle and inducing a constant state of morbid apprehension for your life. This is true. The idea of mixing cars and bicycles together is crazy. Cars themselves are an atavistic idiocy responsible for millions of deaths and injuries. It is entirely logical to want to have nothing to do with them.

On the other hand you can get used to it. If you are an alert, defensive rider you are reasonably safe. In return for the risks there are many benefits and it is up to you to decide how they balance. It isn't all bad by any means, but never deny the stark reality: in traffic there is a chance that you will be killed.

7. Touring and Racing

Touring is the real joy in biking. The only better way to see the country is to walk or roller skate. A bike has advantages in mobility and luggage-carrying however, and the aesthetic sacrifice is not too great. Touring can be done in a tremendous variety of ways. You can go for an afternoon's jaunt or spend a summer or more travelling thousands of miles. You can go as a self-contained unit with your own camping gear, or ultra-light and stay in inns and motels. You can count the miles travelled, or concentrate on the scenery (yeah!). Your journey can include transit by auto, bus, train, boat, and plane, so that you can hop from one interesting place to another. You can have a plan, or absolutely none at all. Touring is a call to adventure, beauty, new sights and experiences.

There's a lot to touring, and plenty for you to think about. At the same time it can be kept simple. Any bike headed for the boondocks should have a tool kit, unless you don't mind pushing your bike a few miles to a garage and/or the possibility of an overnight stay until it opens. Equipment makes a difference, but the main thing is to get out there. My greatest, happiest tour was on a battered 1935 BSA whose vital parts shed like water.

'A merry heart goes all the way,
Your sad tires in a mile, a.'—*Shakespeare.*

73

Part of the fun of touring is figuring it out and planning or not planning for yourself. Some people insist that the only way to tour is with a meticulous and detailed plan; others heave map and compass into the bushes and go wherever fancy takes them. For some the fun and relaxation comes as a result of planned and concentrated effort; for others it is through not thinking about anything. There is no "right" way to tour. Each to his own. Accordingly, this chapter tries to simply give basic information about touring. It is not a step-by-step guide. It's up to you to decide where and when you want to go, and what sort of equipment you expect to need.

One source of detailed information is books. *Bicycle Camping and Touring* (Dell, $3) has a lot of solid information on techniques and equipment. *The Best of Bicycling* (Pocket Books, $1.95) has all sorts of wonderful stories about short and long distance touring and a pot-pourri of technical information. *North American Bicycle Atlas* (American Youth Hostels, $2.25) gives detailed, mapped tours throughout the U.S. of A.

Another good way to get into heavy touring is to join a society or organization. You get a planned tour, the benefit of a group leader who will set a pace within your capacity, and lots of free friendly help and advice. Ride with and get information from:

American Youth Hostels, Inc.
20 West 17th Street,
New York, New York 10011.
A somewhat strait-laced but nevertheless very good outfit with over 4000 hostels in 47 countries, about 100 in the U.S. of A. Good equipment and books. Hostels are sometimes spartan but always serviceable, with fees up to $2. Tours in the U.S. of A. and abroad. Inexpensive.

International Bicycle Touring Society,
846 Prospect Street,
La Jolla, California.
An easy going outfit for adults only. Tours are volunteer organized and fairly luxurious. A sag wagon follows each tour and carries baggage and repair parts. Overnight stays at inns and motels at about $4 to $7.

League of American Wheelmen,
5118 Foster Avenue,
Chicago, Illinois 60630.

An organization founded in 1880 which faded into obscurity but was revived in the 1960 s and has been growing ever since. LAW members are nation-wide, and will give you information about local conditions to aid you in planning a tour. LAW is also into influencing legislative activity, and will give you information on bikeways.

Bicycle Institute of America,
122 East 42nd Street,
New York, New York 10017.

A trade organization which gives out a lot of free information on all aspects of bicycling from car top carriers to bikeways.

Where

Where you go depends on your own temperament, interests, physical conditions, and available equipment. I would suggest that you make your initial rides about 20 miles or so, and work up to longer tours and overnight stays as you get used to it. If you favor back roads off the beaten track and camping, you are going to have to deal with equipment for both you and the bike; touring on better roads and sleeping in inns means less and lighter equipment.

Riding

Safety

I recommend taking the smallest, least travelled roads practicably possible. Not only are they almost always more interesting, but the fewer cars there are around the more comfortable you will be. Cars in the country are a serious hazard because a bicycle rider is a completely unexpected phenomenon for most drivers, and they are not prepared to drive in a fashion safe for you, the cyclist.

Safe country riding is largely a matter of common sense. Most of the rules for traffic riding apply here also.

◎ The cardinal rule is "what if?" Look and think ahead. Don't, for example, time your riding so that you and an overtaking car reach a curve at the same time. If a car — or worse yet a truck — comes the other way there just isn't going to be enough room.

◎ Bear in mind the tremendous relative velocity of cars. In

traffic you can pretty much keep up, but in the country cars will have up to 70 mph over your 5 to 15. If you crest a hill for example, and there is no oncoming traffic, move over into the opposite lane for a while. This avoids the hazard of overtaking cars who cannot see you over the crest.

◉ Try to have a hole to duck into should everything go wrong. Where will you go if that tractor pulls out? If a car comes around the corner on your side of the road are you going to try for the ditch or a tree? You may wreck a bike going off into a field, but this is a lot better than colliding with a car. Think about this as much as you can and try to make it an automatic process. This way when an emergency arises instead of freezing in panic you may be able to save your life.

◉ Rural farm traffic is a law unto itself. Many farmers operate machinery on local public roads as if they were in the middle of a field.

◉ Watch for loose gravel, dirt, or sand, and especially at driveway and side road entrances.

◉ Bridge gratings, cattle guards, railroad tracks, etc. can all swallow up a bicycle wheel and send you flying.

◉ Dogs. Dogs and other creatures of the field and air are a menace to the cyclist. I was once attacked by a determined and large goose. Dogs are the main problem though, and you need to keep a constant lookout for old Towser.

There are many theories about why dogs attack two-wheeled vehicles. I think that the spokes make a noise which drives them nuts. There are also a number of dog owners who take a not-so-secret pleasure in having vicious attack-prone animals, and others who should not even try to take responsibility for a cockroach. One couple expressed puzzlement to me after their dog bit my riding companion: every time the dog was disobedient they said, they beat it until their arms hurt. Why wouldn't it obey? With treatment like that, any dog will become vicious and irrational.

If you can do it, the best thing by far is to outrun an attacking dog. Often this is not possible, but 99 times out of a 100 there is still no serious problem. Many cyclists become hysterical on the subject of dog defense, and recommend whips, car aerials, clubs, and other weapons that will really hurt a dog. This is not necessary. It really isn't the dog's fault. Nine times out of ten he is normally friendly. All you have to do is stop, dismount, and face him directly.

That's all. Simply stop. Often he will come up wagging his tail. When you leave, walk away like all "normal" (to the dog) people do, and the matter will be forgotten.

The tenth time, when a dog still threatens attack: the main thing when dealing with a vicious dog is to have *confidence*. As a human being you are one of the largest mammals on earth and a formidable contender in a fight. Suppress your fears and radiate the notion that any dog that messes with you will regret it for the rest of his days, if he lives that long. It is only the rarest of dogs that will attack a human obviously prepared for self-defense. Speak to the dog in firm tones, keep your bike between you, and slowly walk away.

If the dog attacks: an effective defense are aerosol pepper sprays (hardware stores) made for exactly this purpose. They have a range of about 10 feet and are light enough to clip to the handlebars or your belt. A water pistol loaded with a water ammonia solution will also work, but is a good deal less convenient. If you have neither of these and can't or won't climb a tree get a stick or large rock. No? The bicycle pump. Try to ram it down his throat. In any event, don't cower or cover up, because the dog will only chew you to ribbons. *Attack*. Any small dog can simply be hoisted up by the hind legs and his brains dashed out. With a big dog you are fighting for your life. If you are weaponless try to tangle him up in your bike and then strangle him. Kicks to the balls and which break ribs are effective. If worst comes to worst, ram your entire arm down his throat. He will choke and die. Better your arm than your throat. You can avoid this problem by carrying pepper spray.

If you are bitten and the dog gets away, make every effort to find the dog and owner. If the dog cannot be quarantined you will have to get a long series of painful rabies shots. Ask around the area, check with local gas stations, stores, etc. In any event, get immediate medical treatment, even for a light bite. Then notify the dog warden or police of the incident. If the dog owner is unco-operative about paying for the doctor and any other related expenses, just get a lawyer. The law is completely and absolutely on your side.

If you successfully fend off an attack, notify the dog owner and dog warden or police. This is a very real responsibility because the next person might not be as well prepared as you. A little girl for example, like the one three dogs down the road from my parents' place pulled down and killed a few summers ago.

Technique

Cadence (see   p. 60 for basics)   plays an extremely significant part in the technique of long-distance touring. In a short sprint you can drain your body's resources and strength, but on a long tour output must not exceed ability to continuously replenish fuel and oxygen. Which makes it sound simple: just take it easy and have something in reserve. Not quite.

If you are interested in covering a lot of ground (not everybody is) and in feeling comfortable, then you must strive for an exact balance between energy output and the body's ability to synthesize and store energy. There is a *pace* which works best. Go too fast and the result will be fatigue and possibly strained muscles that will dog you throughout the tour. But go too slow, and you will become sluggish and lethargic, and mistake this for genuine tiredness.

A rough indicator of pace is respiration and heartbeat. You simply cannot sustain for long periods effort which noticeably increases either. Thus, the exact pace you can maintain depends on your physical condition, not on your strength.

I particularly recommend that you take it easy at first, sticking to the lower gears and not pushing hard against the pedals. This will help you to find your own cadence and pace, and perhaps avoid

excessive initial effort. Most people tend to lean into it hard the first day. The result is strained and sore muscles, and the next day they can hardly move. You'll go farther and faster if you take it easy at the start.

Riding position can make a tremendous difference. Going into the wind try to get low down. With a strong tail wind straighten up and get a free push. In Europe many riders use home-made "sails" resembling kites strapped to their backs. These are effective even with a quartering wind. Position determines the muscle groups in use: hands high on the bars eases the back, stomach, arms, and hands; down positions do exactly the opposite and are best for hill climbing.

Equipment

Bike: Can be done on a 3-speed but don't try to cover a lot of ground. You'll be packing an extra 15-20 pounds and working through an inefficient gear train. A 10-speed is the best choice by far. Experienced tourists sometimes prefer 15-speed bikes, but for the tyro these have mechanical problems which offset the advantage of extra gears. Be sure to gear for the terrain you will encounter (pp. 49, 56).

Tires: Tubular tires are fragile and fast. Although on the road a tubular can be changed quickly, they are time-consuming to repair. In the hands of an expert they will give reasonable service and fast running, but tyros should start out on clinchers. These are more durable, easy to repair, and only fractionally slower. Tubulars for point to point speed runs, clinchers for back road meandering, and heavy-duty in either case.

Tool kit:
Tire tools (clinchers)
Tire repair kit
6″ adjustable wrench
Screwdriver
Chain tool
Spoke wrench
Spare chain links
Brake pads
Valve stem
Brake cable

Derailleur cable
Lubricant
Pump

Sounds like a lot, but it all packs into a very compact bundle. If you are 2 or more, back off on the number of spare parts, and share one set of tools.

Fenders: A great pleasure in wet going and rough back roads. Alloy fenders are available for permanent installation, and easily attached and removed plastic models for double-duty machines. Fenders are unnecessary for fast runs and dry weather.

Bicycle shoes and cleats: Used in conjunction with toe clips these are essential for any long-distance travelling, unless you plan to be on and off the bike frequently. Pack along shoes for walking as bicycle shoes are very unsuitable for this.

Baggage: Loading a touring bike is an art. There are two cardinal principles, load low and load evenly. Piling gear up in a high stack or all in one place creates tremendous instability for the bike. Bicycle carriers are designed to distribute loads properly. There are 3 basic kinds: handlebar bags, saddlebags, and panniers. People travelling light can get by with a saddlebag. These fasten to the seat and seat post and can hold a lot of gear. The next addition would be a handlebar bag. This makes for good fore and aft weight distribution, and is handy for food, cameras, and other things you need often. Get one with a transparent map case and that opens forward for easy accessibility. Campers will want rear panniers hung on special frames alongside the wheel. Panniers both front and rear are just too much baggage. Front panniers also stiffen steering and do not have the carrying capacity of rear panniers.

Bike stores and groups like American Youth Hostels sell this sort of equipment, and you can also order it by mail. Deluxe gear is available from:

Gerry
5450 North Valley Highway
Denver, Colorado 80216

Bellweather
1161 Mission St.,
San Francisco, California 94103

Touring Cyclist Shop
Box 378
Boulder, Colorado 80302

Prices are steep but equipment is first-rate. Whatever kind of equipment you use, load evenly and low. Put heavy gear at the bottom, light bulky stuff like sleeping bags at the top. Give yourself a few local shakedown trial runs. The extra weight takes getting used to, and nothing is quite so irritating as rebuilding a luggage rack with inadequate tools in the middle of a tour.

Maps: A compass is not only useful in conjunction with a map, but can itself guide you in the general direction you want to go without strict routing. Sometimes it is fun to dispose of maps altogether. Just go where fancy takes you, and ask directions along the way. You get to meet people, and often they can suggest really interesting routes, scenic attractions, swimming holes, and the like. But have a map in reserve.

As well as keeping you on a desired route, maps have the vital function of keeping you off main travelled roads and out of industrial areas. Of gas station maps I have found Esso's to be the most detailed, but even these do not meet the needs of the cyclist. The best source is the U.S. Geological Service, who publish contour maps for each state. If you know the exact area you'll be in, they also have local maps down to 1:24,000, a scale which shows walls, foot-paths, tiny streams, etc. These are too detailed for any but the most local use, but are extremely interesting. Many map stores carry the U.S.G.S. maps, or you can order them direct (for local maps ask first for free state index map):

East of the Mississippi	West of the Mississippi
U.S. Geologic Survey	U.S. Geologic Survey
Washington District Section	District Section
1200 South Eads Street	Federal Center
Arlington, Virginia 22202	Denver, Colorado 80225

Clothing: Wash and wear is a must for long jaunts. A nylon wind-shirt is very useful, as are cycling jerseys with big pockets for stashing gear. A poncho can serve also as a groundsheet and/or a tent.

Camping gear: Personal preferences and abilities can completely determine choices here. Some people need a tent and a prepared campsite with running water. Others insist on portable stoves, radios, etc. There are many good books on camping equipment and woods lore, and if you are unfamiliar with this craft you should get one. There is space here for only the most generalized suggestions.

1. Sleeping bag. Tents and stoves, etc. can always be improvised with fair success, but only the most skilled can keep warm in a bad bag. A poor bag weighs more, and if you freeze and can't sleep, this will give you ample time to brood on the economic and practical merits of having gotten something that would do the job in the first place. Get the best bag you can afford. Also, although your bike has carrying capacity and most of your touring is apt to be in warm weather, I suggest you keep other possibilities such as backpacking, or tours in the autumn (fantastic!) in mind.

The best bags, pound-for-pound, are of down. Down has the greatest range (temperatures at which the bag will work), resiliency (bag packs small), recovery (gets loft back when unpacked), wicking properties (carries moisture away from body), and moral character. Down bags run from $50 to $125 and the less expensive, lighter (filled with $1\frac{1}{2}$-$2\frac{1}{2}$ pounds of down) models are OK for warm weather. I suggest a multi-layered and/or openable bag that will also take a flannel insert. This gives optimum range and comfort.

An interesting new insulative material is poly foam, used in Ocaté bags. These are only fractionally heavier ($4\frac{1}{2}$ pounds overall) than lightweight down bags ($3\frac{1}{2}$ pounds), and the manufacturer claims a degree range down to $-5°$, about that of a middleweight down bag (4-$4\frac{1}{2}$ pounds). The advantage is that it will keep you warm wet or dry.

The least expensive bags contain synthetic fillers such as 'Dacron 88' and 'Astrofill.' These run from $15 to $40, weigh about 6 pounds, and are OK for warm weather and low altitudes.

2. A ground sheet such as a triple-purpose (raincape, tent) poncho.

The remaining equipment listed here can always be improvised. The trouble with this is that garnering boughs for a bed or building fires is rather wasteful and ecologically unsound. There are enough campers now so that the total destruction can be devastating. In many areas you are not allowed to do these things. So, drag that it may be, it is both practical and considerate to be as self-sufficient as possible.

3. Sleeping mattress or pad. Air mattresses (avoid plastic ones) are comfortable but bulky. Pads such as ensolite are fine.

4. Tents come in all shapes, sizes and grades. Conditions and

personal preference dictate choice. Tents are good for protection against bugs, rain, and to ensure privacy. For myself I see no point in hieing to the Great Outdoors and then sleeping in a dark hole. Polyethylene fly sheets can be rigged into a decent shelter with only a little effort and are extremely cheap and light. A poncho is just as good. In tents the Gerry 'Pioneer' is well thought of by everybody. This makes up as a one-man tent with floor and mosquito netting, or as a two-man tent without a floor.

Gerry
5450 North Valley Highway
Denver, Colorado 80216

5. Cooking stove and utensils. You should have, but I don't know anything about them. Four skewers can be used to form a grid for a pot, a grill, to skewer food, or as tent pegs. Heavy-duty aluminum foil will make a flat-folding re-usable pot.

6. Food. Freeze-dried light-weight foods are extremely convenient and quite palatable. I suggest carrying enough for emergencies only however, and trying for fresh food along the route. Stock up on breakfast and dinner at about 4 o'clock. Mixtures of dried fruit, nuts, grains, dried milk, yeast, etc. are nourishing, tasty, and easy to carry.

Most any city has a camping equipment store. Mail order outfits I have done business with to complete satisfaction are:

L. L. Bean
Freeport, Maine 04032
Not deadly cheap, but always quality equipment which *works*.

Herter's
Route 1
Waseca, Minnesota 56093
Catalog – $1.
My favorite. Chest-thumpers, but sound equipment at very low cost.

Recreational Co-op 1525 11th Street
Seattle, Washington 98122
Excellent equipment at good prices, with a 10% dividend at the end of the year. Nice knapsacks. Costs $1 to join.

Gerry
5450 North Valley Highway Denver, Colorado 80216
Expensive, but first-rate equipment which works really well.

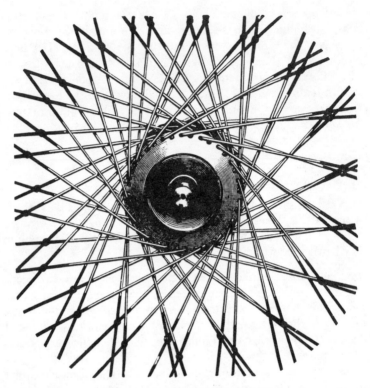

NEW RAPID TANGENT WHEEL.

Getting There

Other forms of locomotion complement bicycles very well.

Cars. A 10-speed with the wheels off will fit in the trunk of many economy cars and certainly on the back seat. For carrying several bikes you can buy or make a car carrier. There are two types, rear end and top. The rear end version holds 2 bikes and is easy to load. It is hard to get at the trunk however, and the bikes get a lot of road grit and scratch each other. A popular model is Bike Toter, about $16 in bike stores or direct from:

Bike Toter
Box 888
Santa Monica, California 90406

Top mounted carriers hold 4 to 5 bikes, and require that each bike be strapped down. But machines are kept clean, separate, and out of harm's way. A deluxe model is available from

JC-1 Industries
904 Nogales Street
Industry, California 91744
$29.95

Most any auto store has luggage racks for about $15 which can easily be adapted for bikes. Or you can make your own, and have something exactly suited for the job. *Bicycle Camping and Touring* (Dell, $3) has plans, and so does

Bicycle Institute of America
122 East 42nd St.,
New York, New York 10017
(free)

When loading, alternate direction for 3 or more bikes. Seat on one cross-bar, handlebars on the other. Careful of brake and shift cables. Lash down with toe straps or elastic luggage straps at contact points, and especially the handlebars, since these hold the bike upright. Guying, running straps from the side of the car to high points on the bike (like with a sailboat mast), is a *good idea*.

Mixing up a tour with public transportation, or even just complementing a trip with a bicycle, is a great way to travel. You get the benefits of mobility and covering a lot of ground, but at the same time a bike lets you examine interesting areas in detail. Preparation of your bike for travel depends on the kind of carrier you will use.

Airlines: These handle bikes well and some, like United, provide special bike boxes. Remove the rear derailleur (p. 224) if you have one, and loosen stem (p. 145) and twist handlebars parallel with front wheel. They may ask you to remove or reverse the pedals (p. 181). I myself would protect the frame and chainwheel with a broken-up cardboard box. Deflate tires to $\frac{1}{2}$ pressure. Airlines sometimes let bikes on free, and sometimes charge.

Buses: Here your bike lies flat on its side in a luggage compartment with a lot of other junk that can bang into it. I strongly recommend picking up a box from a local bike dealer and stuffing yours inside. If you are leap-frogging, send the box on ahead.

Railroads: In Europe you can load a bike into the baggage compartment yourself. In the U.S. of A. the make-work contingent has rigged it so a baggage handler must do the job — badly. Stories of bikes mangled into oblivion by baggage handlers are legion. Insist on personally supervising loading or don't go. Hang the bike from the ceiling or side of the baggage car if possible, and in any case see that it is lashed down securely and that no heavy stuff can fall on it.

Boats: Same story. One boat-loading crew broke an internal gear on a motorcycle of mine. I still haven't figured out how.

Racing

Bicycle racing is quite specialized and involved. Space and my own limited knowledge of the subject permit only the briefest comments and descriptions. For further information I suggest the chapter on racing in Eugene Sloane's *The Complete Book of Bicycling* (Trident Press $9.95); *Cycling*, edited by David Saunders (Wolfe Publishing, available from Foyles, 119 Charing Cross Road, London WC2, England); and *Cycle Racing* by Bowden and Matthews (Temple Press, 42 Russell Square. London WC1, England).

Probably the quickest way to get into a racing scene is to join the Amateur Bicycle Institute of America

4233 205th Street

Bayside, Long Island, New York.

This is the official organization governing racing in the U.S. of A. They will refer you to a local ABA official who will help you get started.

The demands of racing are rigorous. Most racers are not interested in touring because it is not hard enough exercise. Any serious racer has to keep fit with a year-round physical conditioning program. Traffic jammers however, may find that they are part-way conditioned for sprinting. Road, track, and cyclo-cross are the three chief types of races.

Road

Time trial – Rides against the clock over 10, 25, 30, 50, or 100 mile courses in which pure riding ability counts.

Massed start —Everybody starts together, first man over the finish line wins. The course can be 10 miles, or 2,600, as in the Tour de France. Races which last 2 days or more are called stage races. In the massed start riders are pitted against each other, and the resulting shenanigans are sometimes incredible. Teams work together to launch a strong teammate ahead of the pack to victory,

THE 'XTRAORDINARY BICYCLE.

and block opposition riders. In big races like the Tour de France bicycles collide and pedals jam into spokes. In Europe these races go on despite wars, revolutions, or anything else, and are the subject of intense interest. Bikes are of a conventional design, with freewheels and brakes.

Cyclo-cross

Cross-country races from point to point or around a course, from 1 to 16 miles in length. These are typically through steep climbs and descents, mud, thick woods, streams, and hurdles. Some sections have to be negotiated on foot. Bikes are of course somewhat special, with knobby tires and waterproof brakes.

Track

The machine common to a wide variety of track events is the greyhound of bikes: an ultra-light frame with a short wheelbase; a fierce position with the saddle high and handlebars low; a single fixed wheel gear, with no brakes; and tires bonded to the rims with shellac, to withstand the stresses of violent track maneuvers. There are no quick release hubs, gears, pumps, cables, etc., making these among the most lovely and functional of bikes.

There are many different kinds of track events. Here are a few:

Sprint — Usually a 1000 meter course with only the last 200 meters timed. Involves all kinds of tricky tactics and scheming. There are times when racers hold their bikes stock still while jockeying for position. *Behind* the leader and in his slipstream until the final dash is the favored winning position.

Pursuit — Two riders or teams start on opposite sides of the track and try to catch each other.

Time Trials — Against the clock, as in road racing.

Devil Take the Hindmost — Last man over the line every 2 or 3 laps is out.

THE FINISH

8. Accessories

Most accessories are unnecessary. Whenever possible try to peel weight off your bike. Streamers, doodads, and various decorative garb are out, unless they are of such incredibly redeeming character as to make them worth carrying at any cost. I had a Bombay Taxi Driver's Horn like that once, a great gleaming diesel-like trumpet, but it went with the Golden Flash.

Pump — A necessity for tubular tires, an excellent idea for clinchers. City riders can't use them around town, but should on long tours and late night rides.

Toe clips — These nearly double pedalling efficiency and with smooth-soled shoes the feet can be slipped out easily in an emergency. See Riding, pp. 57-61, and Fitting, pp. 45-56.

Bicycle shoes and cleats — These are cut for ankling and have a steel shank for even foot pressure on the pedal. Cleats will give you tremendous get up and go and are a must for long tours and racing.

Lights — A peculiar problem In many areas you are required to have them. They are even useful at times.

There are two kinds of lighting systems: battery and generator. Generator types take power off the wheel and this is precisely the problem. Plus they work only when you are under way, there is more hardware, wires, etc. Battery types all tend to be of the cheapest possible manufacture. There isn't one to recommend. Sorry, but you will have to fight into working condition whatever lights you acquire.

I prefer a portable battery light which slides onto a clip mounted on the handlebars or stem. This way there's no dead weight to lug around during the day, nothing for sticky fingers to dismember, and a free flashlight. For around town use the best bet is a French flashlight with a white front and a red back that straps to the arm or leg. It weighs only 5 ounces and the resulting show is pretty good (bike stores).

Often it will appear pointless to have lights. Most times you can see better without them. Lights are not so much that you see, as that you are seen. A moonlit road in the middle of nowhere is a perfect place for a *car* to run without lights. As I found out. Have some kind of a light. Use it.

Carrier — The best sort of carrier depends on your needs. A cloth rucksack can go with you on and off the bike and is handy while

shopping. For around town use the light aluminum Swiss jobs fitting over the rear wheel and clamping to the back seat stays are excellent (bike stores). For heavier going a steel rack designed for use with panniers is probably best (ditto). See p. 82 for additional information.

Nail pullers — Half-ounce gizmos that ride along above the tire and brush-off shards of broken glass, etc. For tubulars only.

Baby-seats — The only kind worth considering put the child behind the rider and have full leg shields to prevent toes from bloodying spokes.

Fenders — Tourists and people living in rain forests need them. Everybody else, no.

Locks — See Keeping your bike, p. 42 .

Horns — Yelling is the quickest, most reliable, and colorful. Little bells and squeeze horns are forever failing or being vandalized. Freon horns are wonderfully loud — excessively so.

Helmet — Sure. Also full leathers, boots . . .

Feeder bottle — If you're worried about a drink . . .

Kickstands, odometers, speedometers, chain guards — no.

ELLIOTT QUADRICYCLE.

Book Two

1. Maintenance and Repair

Maintenance Program

The subject of maintenance and repair of bicycles is usually clouded with negative feelings. It is regarded as something in the "must be done" category and approached as a chore. Bicycle repair books are fond of saying that any cretin can understand how to fix his machine, or that the book itself has the answer to any problem that might conceivably come up. Both approaches underestimate the reader's intelligence and compartmentalize maintenance and repair, keeping it separate from "riding". This is a basic mistake. The extent to which you get involved in working on your bike should be a direct function of how you ride. One follows the other like night and day. The awareness that riding a bike precipitates usually includes an awareness and interest in the bike itself. How the bike responds is very much a function of maintenance. Ideally, you are going to work on your own bike because you want a together, tight machine under you, i.e., you will do it because *you want to*.

As with all things, you get back in proportion to what you put in. It is essentially a question of fineness. It is the nature of bikes that they are at their best when well-lubricated and carefully adjusted. A sensitivity to this sort of refinement does not happen the instant you mount a bike. Give it time. As you ride you will become increasingly aware of your bike's mechanical characteristics. A well set-up bike fits you like a suit of clothes, and you will soon develop an "ear" for the sound of bearings and a "feel" for other parts, such as the brakes. The development of this sensitivity — the result of personal and direct participation — is part of the reason for owning a bike in the first place. Eventually, you will find that increased riding pleasure is not just a reward for doing your own maintenance, the mechanical sensitivity itself becomes part of the riding pleasure.

As I say, this is all something that you should grow into. The idea of having a bike is to have fun. A fair amount of latitude is possible in servicing bikes and you have hopefully chosen a machine suited to your level of interest. So you can minimize or maximize maintenance as per your own inclinations. But bear in mind that most machines, and certainly bicycles, need a certain amount of lubrication and adjustment if they are to function at all. Without it, they rust away, and because the parts are unlubricated and out of kilter, they slowly chew themselves to bits when ridden. I have seen "old dependables" that have been left out in the rain for years and have never seen an oil can or a mechanic. They make it for years — and then snap a chain in the middle of a tour or a brake cable at the start of a long hill. Or eventually the rust destroys them. There is no need for this. A properly maintained bike will easily last a lifetime (one of mine was made in 1935 and has seen plenty of hard service to boot). For reasons of simple economy and safety, if you can't be bothered to do routine maintenance then take your machine to a bike shop for servicing at least twice a year.

Bike shops. Alas! There are good ones and bad ones. An excellent reason for doing your own work is that you are apt to do a better and quicker job than the shop. Over 8 million bikes were sold in the U.S. of A. last year. Most stores are so busy selling new machines that service programs are minimal. Customers therefore find service time-consuming, expensive, and frequently not very good. It's a real drag to call for your bike a couple of times and be told it's not ready, the part didn't come, it rained, etc. etc. The general atmosphere in many bike stores is that they are doing you a big favor by helping you at all.

The other side of the coin is that some stores have recognized the need for decent service programs and sell their bikes with service guarantees for one to three years. This means that you can bring the bike in for routine servicing and any breakage not due to normal wear and tear is covered, parts and labor both. The stores that offer this feature are usually large, and with a high volume of sales, so that their prices are perfectly competitive with other stores. Even if you do your own work their guarantee is a nice insurance to have. A good bike store needn't be fancy either. There is a tiny, one-man bike/locksmith shop around the corner from me that does perfectly good work at devastatingly reasonable rates. So look around. You may have one or two bad experiences but should eventually find a reliable shop.

No matter if the shop is good or bad, you can't expect the mechanic to have as much interest in getting things just right as you do. Once you learn the drill you will almost always do a better job. Also, it is time-consuming to leave your bike at the store for three days for work that takes ten minutes to do.

Another important reason for doing your own work is that it makes preventive maintenance almost automatic. Preventive maintenance is replacing parts before they wear out and break, usually at an inopportune time and miles from any bike store. If you are paying attention to the various parts of your bike and keeping it in tune this is pretty much going to happen as a matter of course. In turn, breakdowns and repairs will also be fairly well obviated.

I think this approach is the easiest and the most efficient. I have studied every repair manual I could find. Most stress fixing something *after* it has broken. Even though I know how to fix bicycles most of them lose me right away. Either they are filled with long passages of incomprehensible jargon, or they have computer-programming style directions ("If A, go to page 28 C; if not A, go to B, page 34, then to page 28 D.") designed to reduce you to a mindless automaton.

Here is my approach: each major component system of the bicycle such as brakes, wheels, gears, etc. is broken down into four areas –

How It Works
Routine Adjustments
Replacing Parts
Troubleshooting

The idea is to give you a basic understanding of what is happening – and make you a mechanic! How It Works for each section is required reading. It does no good for you to diddle with this or adjust that if you have no idea of how it works. And if something is broken it is impossible for you to fix unless you know how it works in the first place.

It will help a lot if as you read, you look at and feel the corresponding parts on your bike.

I don't cover everything. One wheel is pretty much the same as another. I have tried to include representative types of equipment currently in use but there are bound to be exceptions. If this happens to you try to find the item in this book which most closely resembles the part you are servicing or fixing. Pay particular attention to *function* and then analyze your own part the same way. This should get you through most anything.

There are also some tasks which are just not worth doing. Getting into the innards of a coaster brake multi-speed hub is one of these. It takes a long, long time and isn't fun at all. Some people may resent these omissions. They want to do everything for themselves.

Well, the point of diminishing returns is reached with attempts to service the coaster brake 3-speed hubs. Even most bike shops refuse to overhaul these units and simply replace them — it's actually cheaper this way. If you insist on doing this sort of work, detailed instructions are available from the bicycle manufacturer or from the hub manufacturer.

Tools

You can get by with amazingly little in the way of tools. However, for some kinds of work there are a few you will just have to get. Also, what you need depends on what kind of bike you have.

Before going into particulars a word on tool quality: do yourself a favor and buy good ones. Dime stores, supermarkets, and even hardware stores carry cheap bargains like 29¢ screwdrivers and $1.00 wrenches. These are a false economy, for they are made of inferior metals that will break or bend under stress, or they are made badly enough so that they don't even work. You do not need many tools, and the total investment should be between $8.00 and $12.00. In the long run it is worth it. I have had the same 8″ adjustable end wrench for 24 years.

Foreign made bikes, and American bikes with foreign components, use metric system nuts and bolts. If you have an all-American bike make the substitutions indicated on the following lists.

For both 3- and 10-speed bikes:
Hardware store
8″ or 6″ Adjustable end wrench.
Pliers.
Hammer.
¼″ tip, 4-5″ shank screwdriver.
⅛″ tip, 2-3″ shank screwdriver.
Wire clippers.
6″ File, mill bastard.
Bike store
Mafac tool kit – contains tire irons, wrenches, other gear, including tire patching kit.
All-purpose tool like Raleigh give-away.
Thin hub wrenches, 13 × 14 and 15 × 16 (Campagnolo preferred).
Spoke wrench.
Pedal wingnut wrench (for pedals with outside dustcap only).

Note: For all of above, substitute U.S. equivalent if you have an American bike.

Tire gauge: for Schrader valve if you have clincher tires.

for Presta valve if you have tubulars.

Tire patch kit for your tires.

10-speed bikes:
Bike store
Chain rivet remover.
Freewheel remover. There are two kinds:

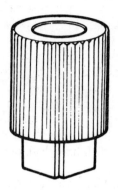 

Look at your freewheel and see if it is splined or not on the interior to see what kind you need.

Set metric allen wrenches (Sears also sells these).

If you have a Campagnolo derailleur, a special Campagnolo combination allen and socket wrench.

If you have cotterless cranks you will need a special crank removing tool as per your brand of crank.

Other useful tools:
Set of wrenches.
Vise-grip pliers.
Channel lock pliers.
Small portable vise.

As you can see from studying the list, many of the tools are for specialized jobs so you do not have to acquire them all at once. Absolutely essential, and especially for trips, is the Mafac toolkit, a screwdriver, and an all-purpose combination tool like the Raleigh give-away.

You will need some means of holding the bike upright with one wheel off the ground. A nail driven into the doorjam with a rope to hang the bike by will do. So will more elaborate arrangements of supporting arms and clamps. Your situation will be the main determinant here — garage, basement, apartment, or whatever — but you will want something.

Lubrication

This is a general discussion of lubrication. For details look under the system in question, e.g. brakes, gears, wheels, etc.

There are three basic types of lubricants:
1. Petroleum distillate sprays such as WD-40 or LPSW-1. These can be used as a substitute for oil, are easy to apply, and most importantly, are clean.
2. Oil. Use only a good grade, non-gumming, such as Sturmy-Archer, or gun oil. Do not use household oils.
3. Bearing grease. Lubriplate and Gold Medal are good brands. Or save money and buy it in an auto store.

Your bicycle has upwards of 200 ball bearings held in place by cups and cones:

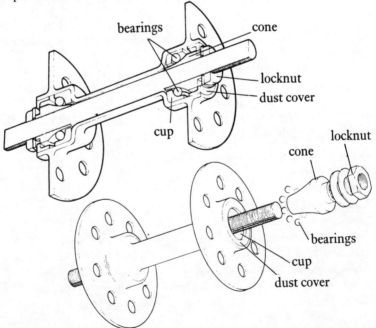

The cone remains stationary while the cup, and whatever part is attached to it — in this example it would be a wheel — rides on the ball bearings and spins around. The distance between the cone and the cup is adjustable and must not be too tight or too loose. Sometimes the ball bearings are held in a clip called a *race*:

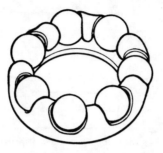

Typically, this is positioned so that the open side through which the balls stick is against the cup. You will find bearings at the headset, bottom bracket, wheels, and pedals:

These bearings are usually disassembled, cleaned thoroughly in kerosene or other solvent, packed with grease and reassembled, every six months. See under relevant section for disassembly technique. Some bearings are both greased and oiled, and in particular, 2- and 3-speed hubs and hubs on ultra-fancy racing bikes. You can tell these by the fact that the hub has a small oil cap or clip:

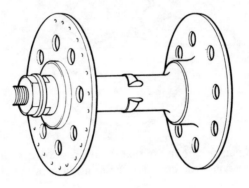

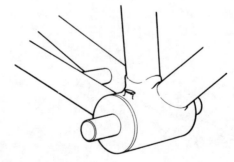

These need oil once a month: multi-speed internal gear hubs a tablespoonful, regular hubs about ½ teaspoonful, and coaster brake hubs 2 tablespoonfuls. Some bottom brackets are set up to use oil. A teaspoonful once a month. Use oil wherever you find oil caps or clips. Do not use spray on these parts as it dissolves the grease.

I greatly prefer the use of petroleum distillate spray like WD-40 or LPSW-1 for the chain, freewheel, derailleur, brake pivots, cables, and any other parts which do not use grease:

The spray is easy to apply with pin-point accuracy, displaces water, and dries clean. This last is really important. The trouble with oil is that it attracts dirt which then mixes with the oil to form a nice gooey abrasive mixture. In the case of the chain, for example, this means that once a month you have to remove it, soak it in kerosene or other solvent, and then oil and install. It's time consuming and messy. If you use spray you need do this job only once every two or three months or even longer if you do not use your bike much. Since the spray goes on in seconds you can lubricate the chain every two weeks. The same rationale applies for the freewheel and derailleur. The spray is particularly useful for the brake pivots and all cables. Oil has a tendency to leak out onto the brake levers and handlebars, and brake shoes. Once a month is sufficient.

If you are on the cheap, paraffin makes a good substitute. You can get it at grocery stores for about 25¢ a bar. Clean your chain in the conventional manner with kerosene or other solvent. Melt the paraffin in a coffee can over the stove. Dump the chain in and then hang to dry so that drippings fall back into can. Use oil or spray for the brake pivot points, freewheel and derailleur. The paraffin will not work well on these parts because it cools and hardens too quickly on contact with the metal to penetrate effectively. It is excellent for brake cables, however. Just run the cable through a block of paraffin a few times until it is well impregnated. Save and re-use the old paraffin. Paraffin, like spray, does not attract dirt.

Note: New bikes fresh from the dealer and bikes that have been standing around for a long time may be dry as a bone. *Oil Evaporates!* Be sure to lubricate such machines before using.

General Words

There are a number of things to keep in mind when servicing bikes:

1. Do not use a great deal of force when assembling or dis-assembling parts. Bicycle components are frequently made of alloys for light weight. These are not as strong as steel and it is not hard to strip threads or otherwise damage parts. Always be sure that things fit. Be careful and delicate. Snug down bolts, nuts, and screws firmly, not with all your might.

2. Most parts tighten *clockwise* and come apart turning *counterclockwise*. This is called a right-hand thread. A left-hand thread tightens *counterclockwise*, and loosens *clockwise*. Left-hand threads are not used often.

3. When fitting together threaded parts hold them as perfectly aligned as you can, and turn one backwards (loosen) until you hear and feel a slight click. Then reverse and tighten. If this is new to you, practice on a nut and bolt until you have the feel of it perfectly.

4. If you get stuck with a rust-frozen bolt or nut, soak it in penetrating oil, give it a few light taps to help the oil work in, and then try to undo it again with a tool that fits exactly. If this fails try a cold chisel and hammer:

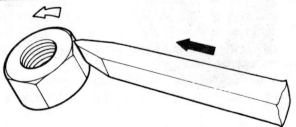

Go at this carefully since if you slip you may gouge a chunk out of your bicycle. If this fails, hacksaw or file the nut or bolt off. How did it get this rusty in the first place?

5. When assembling or disassembling try to be neat and organized. Lay parts out in the order which they came apart or go together. Put tiny parts in boxes or jars.

6. There are a number of little nuts and bolts on your bike for cable clamps, racks, brake lever mounts, gear shift lever mounts, and the like. These tend to get loose and need tightening about once a month.

7. The left side of the bike is as if you and the bike both point forward.

8. Solvents: kerosene and paint thinner are good. Gasoline is very dangerous.

9. Finish: a good quality auto paste wax will preserve your paint job and make it easier to keep clean. Wipe the bike down once a week and after major journeys. Do not wax wheel rims where brake shoes contact.

2. Brakes

Contents / Index

The Brakes

Bicycle brakes come in two basic types: coaster, or pedal-operated, and caliper, or hand-operated. The coaster brake is inferior, because under conditions requiring a quick stop it tends to lock the rear wheel, causing the bike to skid rather than slow down.* It is also extremely difficult to service, and is for the rear wheel only, cutting braking efficiency below 50 per cent, since it is at the front

*A screeching tire-smoking stop is not the quickest. When the wheel is locked, the rubber literally melts into the road, providing a *liquid* point of contact between the tire and road surface, and greatly increasing stopping distance. The quickest stops are done by slowing the wheel to the point just before locking. Skidding also means a loss of directional control and often results in a fall.

wheel that the greatest braking power can be attained. In fact, on dry pavement it is difficult to lock up a front wheel. This is because braking throws the weight forward, increasing traction. If you have a bike which has only a coaster brake at least equip it with a caliper brake for the front wheel. Only children without the necessary strength to operate caliper brakes should have a coaster brake, and they should not ride in any situation requiring quick stops or sustained braking. Lots of the small-wheel hi-riser handlebar banana-seat chopper jobs feature coaster brakes. Kids are fond of diving these bikes into a tight corner, jamming on the brake, and pivoting on the front wheel to come around in a tight, flashy skid. Each to his own, but the same effect can be achieved with a well-adjusted center-pull caliper brake.

If something goes wrong with your coaster brake, simply remove the entire rear wheel (p.159) and take it to a bicycle shop for overhaul or replacement. It is much too complicated to attempt to fix it yourself and infinitely more trouble than it is worth.

How Brakes Work.

Caliper brake systems all work on the same basic principle. There is a hollow, flexible tube called a cable housing between the brake lever mount and the cable hanger:

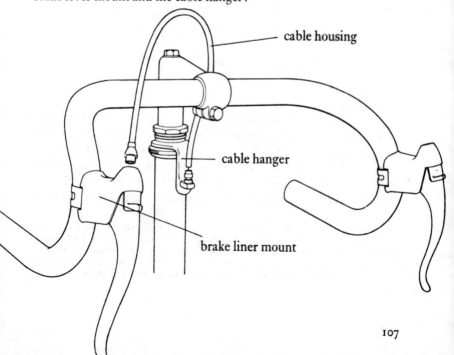

cable housing

cable hanger

brake liner mount

The cable housing is flexible so that the handlebars can turn back and forth. Through the cable housing passes a cable which is attached to the brake lever at one end:

And to the brake mechanism at the other. This is in turn attached to the bicycle frame and functions like a pair of complicated ice tongs with double pivot points. When the brake lever is operated, it pulls the cable through the cable housing and pinches together the arms (called *yokes*) of the brake mechanism, causing the two rubber brake shoes attached to the yokes to press against the wheel rim and stop the wheel:

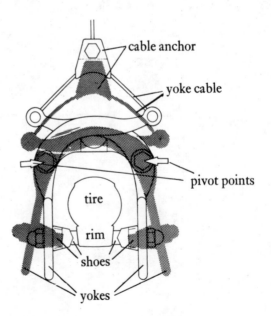

When the lever is released, a spring forces the yoke arms away from the wheel rim:

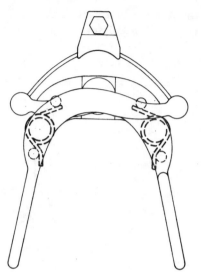

This in turn returns the brake lever to an off position, and keeps continuous tension on the entire brake assembly. This is the basic center-pull mechanism.

The side-pull brake uses only one pivot point, with the cable housing attached directly to one yoke, and the cable to the other. The effect is the same:

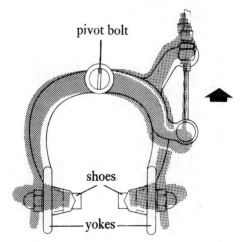

pivot bolt

shoes

yokes

All caliper brake systems have an adjusting screw (called a *barrel adjustor*) for changing the relationship of the cable housing length to the length of the brake cable. On the side-pull brake this is almost always found on the yoke to which the cable housing is attached (A), while on the center-pull brake it is usually at the brake lever (B) or the cable hanger (C):

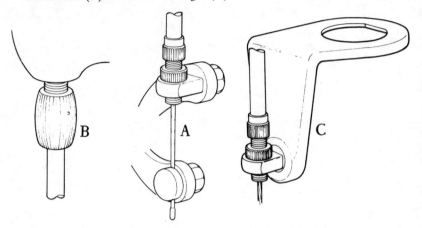

Properly adjusted brake shoes are so close to the wheel rim that the tire will not slide between them when removing the wheel. Accordingly, better grade brake systems have a means for creating a little extra slack in the brake cable. This is usually a small button which allows the brake lever to open more:

button

Or a small cam on the cable hanger:

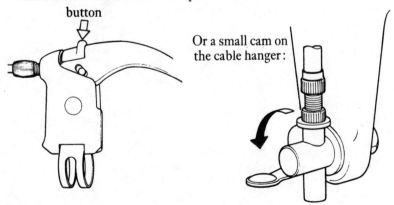

These are the basics of any caliper brake system: a brake lever, a brake cable and housing with adjustor barrel, a cable hanger for center-pull systems, and the brake mechanism, including yokes, springs, and brake shoes. Better systems include either a button or cam to provide extra slack in the cable when removing the wheel or servicing the brakes:

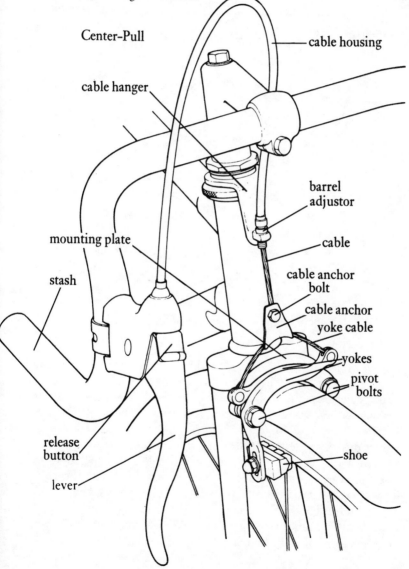

Center-Pull

cable housing

cable hanger

barrel adjustor

mounting plate

cable

stash

cable anchor bolt

cable anchor

yoke cable

yokes

pivot bolts

release button

shoe

lever

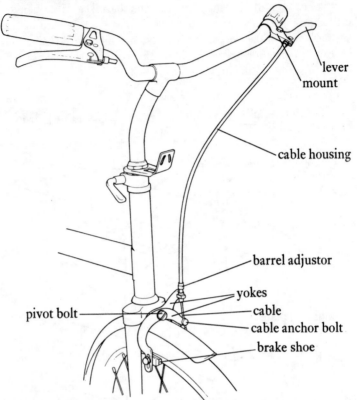

Side-Pull

lever mount

cable housing

barrel adjustor

yokes
cable
cable anchor bolt
brake shoe

pivot bolt

Lubrication

Try to avoid the use of oil. At the brake levers it works out over everything and gets your hands dirty every time you ride. At the brake mechanism it dribbles down to the brake shoes, cutting braking power. A better product is a spray such as WD-40 or LPSW-1, dry film lubricants which displace water and do not attract dirt. Use the little plastic nozzle which comes with the can for pin-point accuracy, and spray pivot bolts, all exposed cable (use a piece of paper or cardboard as a backstop to prevent the spray from going all over the bike), yoke cable anchor points, brake lever pivots, and inside the cable housings. Machines used once or twice a week need lubrication every two months, those in daily use, monthly. More often on tours.

Routine Adjustments

Whatever kind of caliper brake system you have, there are two basic kinds of adjustments: (1) seeing that the brake shoe hits the wheel rim properly, and (2) keeping slack out of the cable between the brake lever and mechanism, so that the lever travels the shortest possible distance when putting on the brakes.

First check to see that the wheel is true by spinning it and seeing that the rim, not the tire, stays about the same distance from the brake shoe all the way around. If play is greater than approximately $\frac{1}{8}''$ the wheel should be trued (see p. 172) before any brake adjustments are attempted. Check also that the wheel is reasonably centered between the fork arms, and that the rim is free of major dents and abrasions. If off center, take the bike to a shop to have the forks checked, and if the rim is badly banged up, get a new one.

Brake shoes: These need to be aligned so that the shoe hits the rim squarely:

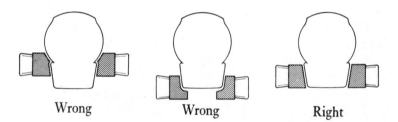

Wrong   Wrong   Right

Brake shoes are held on either by a conventional bolt;

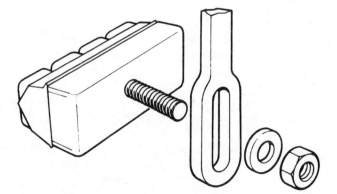

or an eyebolt:

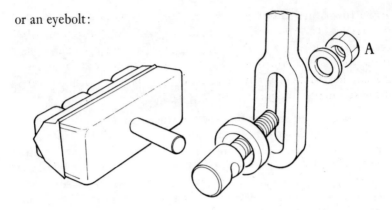

In either case, loosen nut *A*, adjust brake shoe to meet rim, and tighten. One method is to loosen nut *A* just a little bit and gently tap the shoe into the proper position with the wrench handle. With conventional bolts you'll find that the brake shoe twists to the right when you tighten the nut back down. A good trick is to set it slightly counter-clockwise so that the final tightening brings it perfectly into position. Do not use too much force. Brake bolt screws strip easily.

Eyebolt-type shoes are easy to adjust so that the face of the shoe is flush with the rim. Achieving this effect with a conventional-bolt brake shoe sometimes requires bending the yoke. Remove the brake shoe altogether and fit an adjustable end wrench snugly over the end of the yoke:

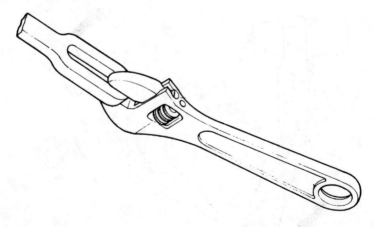

If the yoke needs to be bent outward, simply pull on the handle of the wrench. *Go Slow* – if you break or mangle the yoke you will probably have to get a whole new (expensive) brake mechanism. If the yoke needs to be bent inward, provide a pivot point by wedging another wrench, screwdriver handle, or other object between the yoke and tire, and push on the wrench handle:

If you don't have a suitable wrench, use a screwdriver:

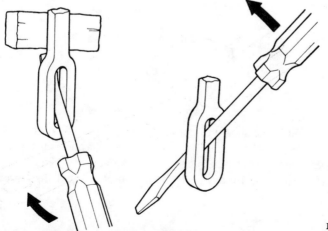

Do not be especially keen to start bending things. New brake shoes, for example, will frequently wear into correct alignment with a few days' use:

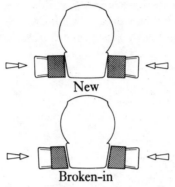

New

Broken-in

Use soft rubber racing-type brake shoes (usually colored red) rather than the hard rubber (usually black) kind typically supplied with side-pull brakes. The soft shoes wear out faster but work a lot better and cost only a few cents each. You can buy the shoes separately from the metal holder and bolt. The holder is open at one end. Slide the old shoe out and the new one in:

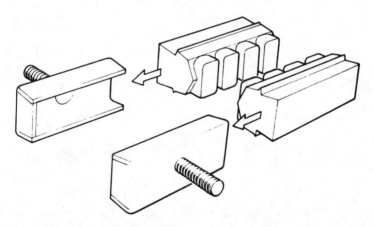

If the old brake shoe will not come out easily and you do not have access to a vise to securely grip the holder while you tap out the shoe, forget it and buy a new set of holders and shoes (about 50 cents each). Be sure to install the new units so that the closed end faces forward (the direction the bike goes), or else the shoes will slide out when the brakes are applied.

Some people consider it good practice to toe-in the fronts of the brake shoes. This is done by twisting the yoke with a wrench or screw driver so that the front of the shoe hits the rim $\frac{1}{32}''$ before the back. Under hard braking however, the whole shoe is flush to the rim. If you have squealing brakes this may cure the problem.

Cables: Once the brake shoes have been properly aligned they should be placed as close to the rim as possible without rubbing when the wheel is spun, $\frac{1}{8}''$ or less. This is done, for both side- and center-pull brakes, with the barrel adjustor and locknut, and the cable anchor nut and bolt:

Barrel adjustor

Cable Anchor Bolt

The idea is to screw in the barrel adjustor, take up as much slack as possible at the anchor nut, and then use the barrel adjustor to take up slack every few days. The cable is always stretching. When the barrel adjustor reaches the limit of its travel, the process is repeated. There are a number of different methods for doing this job, depending on the number and type of tools that you have. A very handy gadget is called a "third hand" and is a spring-like affair for compressing brake shoes together. Bike stores have them. The reason for this tool, or substitute, is that if you just loosen the anchor cable nut the spring tension of the brake yoke arms will pull the cable through and you will have a hard time getting it back in. With or without a third hand:

Undo locknut and screw adjustor barrel all the way in:

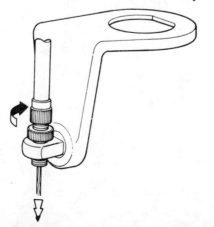

Check and see that the brake release button or cam is set for normal operation (not on all bikes). If you have a third hand, mount it. Or use a C-clamp. Or even string. If you have none of these things, squeeze the brake yoke arms together with your hand. With the other hand, pull the cable at the brake mechanism out so the brake lever is fully home, as it would be if the brakes were not on. Make sure the cable housing has not caught on the outside lip of the barrel adjustor. Now look at the amount of slack in the cable. For center-pull brakes this is the distance between the yoke cable and the cable anchor A :

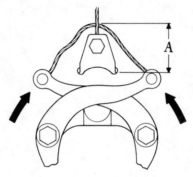

And for side-pull systems, it is the amount of new cable protruding beneath the yoke A :

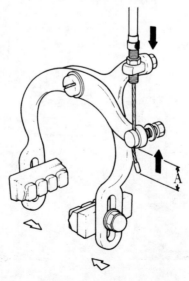

Estimate the amount of slack to be taken up with a ruler, tool handle, or finger. Disengage the yoke cable from the cable anchor (center-pulls) or the cable end from the yoke (side-pulls). Eliminate this step if you have a third hand or similar device. Use two wrenches to slacken the cable anchor nut. Avoid twisting the cable. Pass the cable the required distance through the hole in the cable anchor bolt:

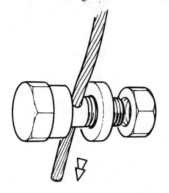

If it is sticky use a pair of pliers to pull it. Tighten cable anchor nut. If no third hand, hold brake yoke arms together again and slip yoke cable back over cable anchor, or cable back into yoke. If you have the feature, now is the time to use the brake button or cam to give you that little bit of extra slack you need. Release the second or third hand, as the case may be. Only one or two turns of the barrel adjustor should bring the brake shoes as close as possible to the wheel rim without actually touching when the wheel is spun. If you have gotten it right (it usually takes a couple of tries), use wire-cutters to snip off the excess cable for a neat job. Frayed cable ends have a habit of snagging fingers and clothing.

SANGER RACER.   AAP

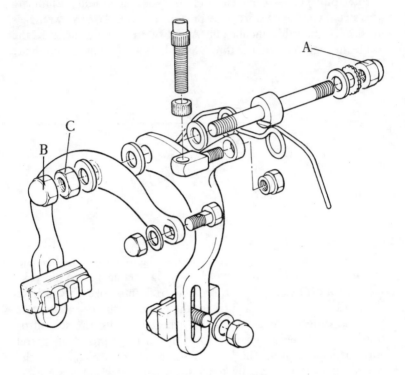

Make sure nut A is tight. Turn in locknut C one half turn while holding acorn adjusting nut B still with another wrench. Turn both B and C in flush against brake yoke arm. Back B off one half turn, hold in place, and lock locknut C against it.

Center-pull brakes: see p. 133.

Replacing Parts

Brake shoes: See p. 116.

Cables:

The frequency with which you will need to replace brake (and other) cables depends on how you use your bike. Machines consistently left out in the rain, or used hard every day, are going to need them sooner than well-cared-for or average-use machines. There is no hard and fast rule. Any obvious defect, such as a frayed cable:

is immediate grounds for replacement, as is stickiness in the motion of the cable through the cable housing (see Trouble-shooting). It is generally good practice to replace both brake cables at the same time. They are cheap, and if one has run its course, it is likely that the other has too. The inconvenience of a broken cable is not worth the gain of a month's extra use. If you have purchased a used bike I would replace cables all around unless you know they are relatively new and obviously in good condition. Good condition means they are clean, have no kinks or frayed spots, and pass easily through the cable housings.

Unless you can specify the brand and model of brake, take your bike or old cable to the store. Cables come in different shapes, lengths, and thicknesses. It is very irritating to discover in the middle of things that you have the wrong part.

I recommend using the right hand brake lever for the rear brake. This follows standard practice, and since the rear brake is generally more favored for routine braking, leaves the left hand free for cross-traffic signals.

For any caliper brake system, first screw home the barrel adjustor:

Center-pulls: push together brake yoke arms (use third hand or similar device if available) and slip yoke cable off brake anchor. Undo cable anchor bolt and nut and slide same off cable:

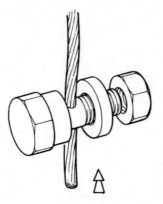

Side-pulls: One kind of side-pull brake uses a cable anchor bolt and nut at the yoke. Slack it off and pull out the cable the same way as with a center-pull. Another type of unit has a ball or nipple on the cable which slips into a slot on the brake yoke arm. You will have to replace both the cable and cable housing as a single unit. Compress brake yoke arms and release ball or nipple from yoke:

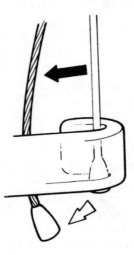

Center-pulls and Side-pulls:
Front brakes: Slide the cable housing off the cable. If yours has ferrules:

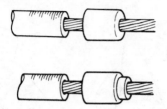

keep track of where they go.

Rear brakes: Leave the housing attached to the frame and pull the cable out of the housing. If you have a one-piece cable and housing (nipples on both ends of the cable), loosen the clamps on the frame and draw the unit through. Examine the cable housings to see if they need replacement. Are they kinked or broken?

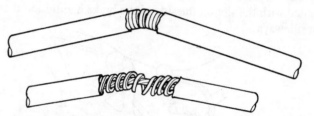

Are the ends free from burrs?

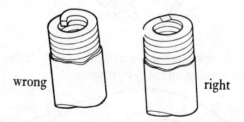

You can eliminate a burr by
(1) snipping off the cable housing end with a strong pair of wire cutters (pliers are not good enough);
(2) clamping the cable housing end in a vise and filing it down; or
(3) by using a tool called a taper ream, which you insert in the cable housing end and twist until the burr is gone.

If you use wire cutters be sure to get the cutting edges in between the coils of the housing or else you will mash the ends flat:

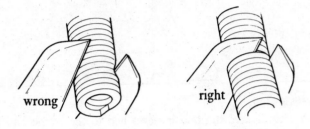

Use this opportunity to lubricate the inside of the cable housing.

Fully depress brake lever. Side-pulls: move cable until it is aligned with the slot on the side of the brake handle and then slide it out sideways:

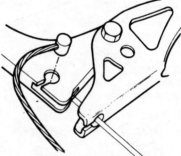

On center-pulls the process is exactly the same, or the slot may be parallel to the cable, as on the Weinmann:

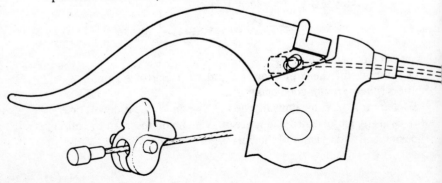

When installing the new cable, save any cutting for last. Cutting invariably frays the cable end and makes it hard to slide through the housing and cable anchor bolt. Installation is the reverse of removal, and for clarification look at the illustrations for that section.

One-nipple cable: Slip cable through brake lever mount and attach to brake lever. Front brakes: including ferrules where used, slip housing on cable. Rear brakes: slide cable into housing. Twist the cable or housing as you do this to avoid catching the cable:

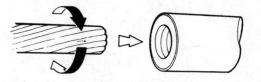

and be sure to do it in the right direction or the cable will unravel. Push free cable end through cable hanger (center-pulls), or through barrel adjustor at yoke (side-pulls), and then through cable anchor bolt hole. To adjust see pp.117-119.

Two-nipple cable (one-piece housing and cable): Attach to brake lever. For rear brakes, slide housing through clamps on frame. Front and rear, pass cable end through barrel adjustor on brake yoke arm and fix to opposite brake yoke arm by slipping ball or nipple into slot. Take up slack with barrel adjustor. Rear brakes, tighten housing clamps on frame, and take care that they are set so clothing will not snag on the screws when riding.

Handles

Outside bolt type:

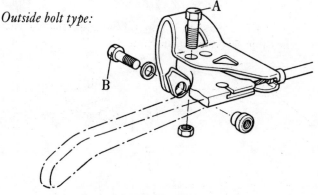

To adjust, slacken A and move. To remove, take off bolt B. May have to be slid back off handlebar in which case grip must be removed. If your brake lever mount has a slot in the bottom:

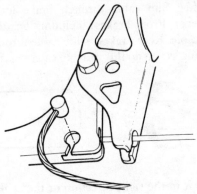

or if the cable ball or nipple will pass through the hole in the mount, then create enough slack by screwing home the barrel adjustor and clamping together the brake shoes, and disconnect the cable from the lever. If this is not possible, then disconnect the cable anchor bolt at the brake mechanism and take the cable out altogether.

Inside bolt type:

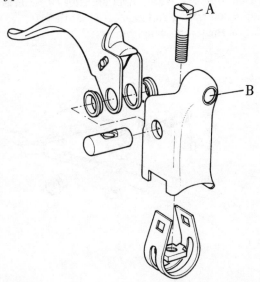

Disconnect yoke cable from cable anchor. Fully depress brake lever and use screwdriver or socket wrench on bolt A. If you are replacing the brake lever, you may need to take out the brake cable (see p. 120). On some systems such as Weinmann the cable end will pass directly through the hole B in the brake mount.

Brake Mechanism

First disconnect brake cable.
Side-pull systems:

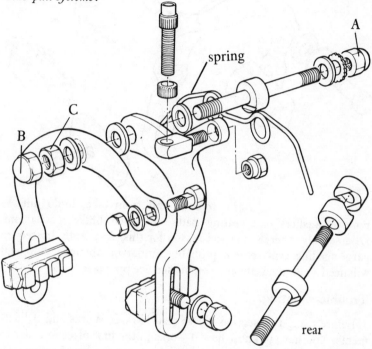

To remove entire brake from bike, undo nut A. Disassembly: should be done only to replace a specific part if it won't work. Start with brake mechanism on bike. Undo the brake spring by prising it off with a screwdriver. Careful of fingers. Separate nut B from nut C, and take them both off the pivot bolt. Then the rest of the stuff. Keep the parts lined up in the order which you remove them. If you are replacing the pivot bolt, undo nut A and take off bolt. Reverse procedure for re-assembly.

Center-pull systems:

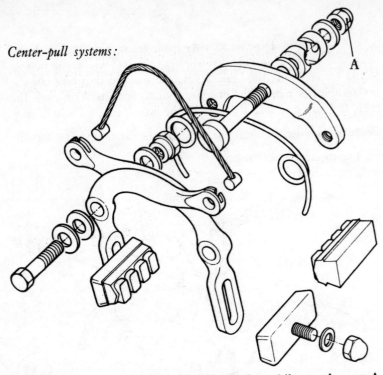

A

        To remove unit from bike, undo nut A, remove washers and seating pads, and then brake mechanism. Disassembly: there's no good reason for this. Any badly busted up parts needing replacement probably cannot be obtained, and you will need a new mechanism. You insist? See pp. 134-5.

Trouble-shooting

Before using this section please read How It Works and Adjustments. You have to know how it works in the first place in order to figure out what's wrong. Brake problems come in 3 broad categories. In each category there are three possible areas in which the trouble may be: brake lever, cable, or mechanism. The first thing is to find in which of these the problem originates, and this is done by isolating and actuating each unit separately.

   Category 1 – No or very weak brakes.

◉ Is rim oily?

◉ Are shoes hitting rim?

◉ Will brake mechanism compress when you squeeze it with your hand? If no, go to Category 3, sticky brakes, below. If yes,

◉ Does lever move freely ? Yes ? Broken cable. Replace.

◉ Lever will not move. Disconnect cable at brake mechanism end. Will cable housing slide off cable ? No ? Cable is frozen inside housing. Get it off somehow and replace. If cable and housing separate easily then,

◉ Lever is frozen. First see if your unit has an adjustable bolt (B)

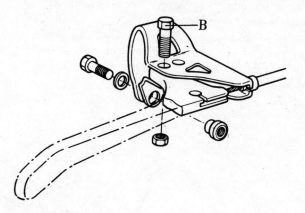

for the lever: and if so give it a try. No ? A major bash may have pinched together the sides of the brake lever mount housing. Examine it carefully and bend out dented parts with a big screwdriver:

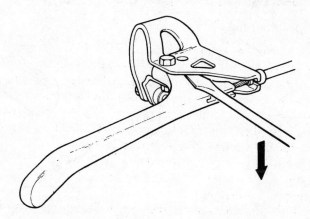

Or the lever itself may be bent. Bend it back. If the bend has been severe replace the lever or unit. Metal which has been bent a lot may look perfectly OK but is fatigued and weak, and may well snap under the pressure of an emergency stop.

Category 2 – Brakes work, but unevenly or make noises.

◉ Juddering. Can be caused by a loose brake mechanism, uneven rims, or sometimes by a very loose headset. To fix the brake mechanism:

Side-pulls. Make sure nut A is tight. Undo locknut C from acorn adjusting nut B and screw both in flush against brake yoke arm. Back off B one half turn and lock in place with locknut C. (see opposite page)

Center-pull

A

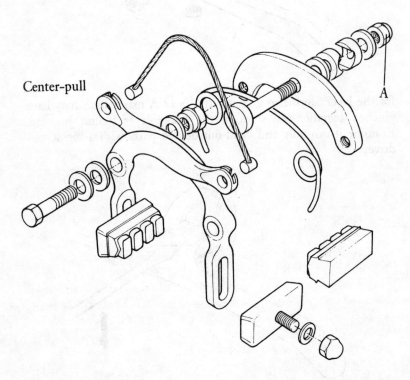

Center-pulls. Tighten up nut A on the mounting bolt.

◎ Squealing. Brake shoes may be old and hard. Sometimes rubber from shoes has streaked rim. Clean with a strong solvent like benzene or cleaning fluid in a WELL VENTILATED AREA. Squealing brakes can sometimes be fixed by toeing in the brake shoes (see p. 117), and sometimes this problem just can't be eliminated.

Category 3 – Sticky or dragging brakes.

This is the most common problem. First determine if it is the lever, cable, or mechanism which is at fault.

◎ If it is the lever, see Frozen lever p. 129.
◎ If it is the cable, replace it (pp. 120–125).
◎ Brake mechanism.

Side-pulls:

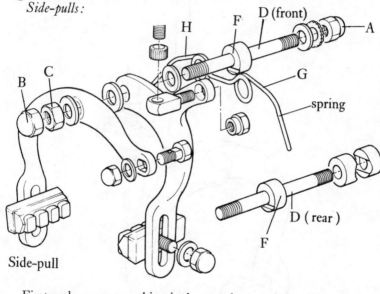

Side-pull

First make sure everything is there and properly hooked up. This sounds simple-minded, but there is a reason for each of the parts and the mechanism won't work without them. Is the spring complete and attached to both yoke arms? Make sure nut A is tight. Undo locknut C from acorn adjusting nut B and screw both flush against yoke arm. Back B off one half turn and lock with C. Check that pivot bolt D is straight and replace if necessary. Lubricate.

If one shoe drags against rim: loosen the mounting nut A, hold brake yokes in correct position, and re-tighten. No soap? Examine brake seating pad F. If it has a slot for the spring you will have to try bending the spring. There are two ways to do this. One is to prise the spring arm off the brake yoke which is dragging and bend it outward using pliers or similar tool. The second is to take a big screwdriver and poise the end against point G or H, whichever is *opposite* the dragging shoe, and give it a sharp bash with a hammer. This second method is quicker, but of course a little riskier.

Still no soap? Check to see that the brake yokes are not rubbing against each other. If so, bend them apart with a screwdriver:

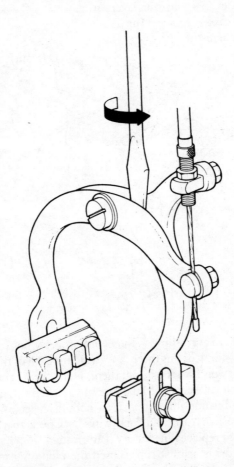

or slide in a piece of fine emery cloth (like sandpaper) and file it down.

If this is not the problem and you have tried everything else a complete disassembly (see p. 127) is necessary. Study each part to see if it obviously needs replacing (like a washer bent out of shape). It may be that the yokes cannot rotate on the pivot bolt. File down and polish the bolt, or enlarge the holes in the yokes (with a taper ream, or emery cloth wrapped around a nail). If none of these things work get a new brake mechanism.

Center-pulls:

Center-Pull

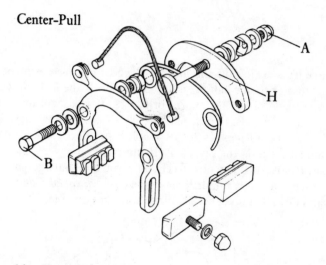

Is cable adjusted correctly?

Are all parts there? Is spring intact and properly mounted?

Is mounting nut A tight?

If one shoe is dragging against rim, slack off A, center brake mechanism, and re-tighten A.

If both shoes stick try lubricating the pivot bolts B while wiggling the yokes back and forth. No? You will have to get into the pivot bolts.

First disconnect the spring. Study the bolts to see if they are type 1, where the pivot bolt screws into the brake arm bridge H; type 2, where the pivot bolt screws into a post which comes off the brake arm bridge and on which the yoke rotates; or type 3, where the pivot bolt simply goes through the brake arm bridge and the yoke rotates on a bushing.

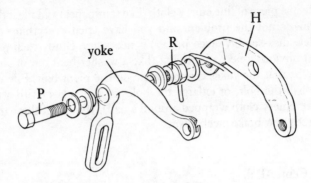

Type 1:

First try slacking off the locknut R and undoing the pivot bolt P one quarter to one half turn. On some models the locknut R is on the other side of the brake arm bridge H. If yoke will now pivot, retighten locknut R. If not, remove pivot bolt P altogether. Keep track of all the washers. Is the pivot bolt P straight? Look for dirt or scarred surfaces on the pivot bolt P and inside the yoke. Clean and polish. If yoke will not turn freely on pivot bolt, enlarge yoke hole with a taper file or ream, drill, or emery cloth wrapped around a nail. Or sand down the pivot bolt. Lubricate and reassemble.

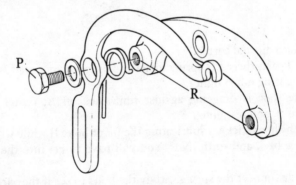

Type 2:

Undo spring and remove pivot bolt P. Remove yoke and keep track of washers. Check for grit and clean. Is post R scarred? Polish with fine sandpaper or steel wool until yoke will rotate freely on it. Lubricate and reassemble.

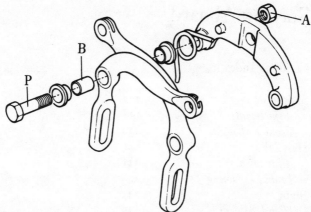

Type 3:

Undo nut A and remove pivot bolt P. Keep track of bushings and washers. Is pivot bolt straight? Is bushing B in good condition? Check for grit and clean. If yoke still sticks, try polishing pivot bolt with steel wool. Lubricate and reassemble.

3. Staying Aboard

Contents/Index

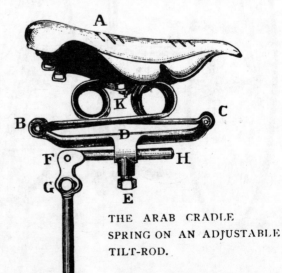

THE ARAB CRADLE
SPRING ON AN ADJUSTABLE
TILT-ROD.

Saddle

There are two important factors in bicycle saddle design: supporting weight, and reducing friction between the legs. The mattress saddle used on bikes with level handlebars has to support all of the weight of the rider, and is therefore usually wide, and equipped with coil springs:

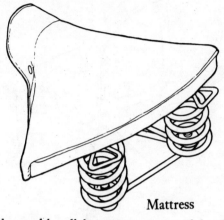

Mattress

Bikes with dropped handlebars support part of the rider's weight on the bars, and can use a long, narrow seat which minimizes friction between the legs:

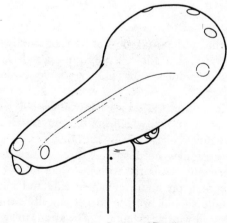

Racing

Adjustments

Springiness in the narrow racing saddle should be kept to a comfortable minimum as it adversely effects pedalling power. If yours is too tight or loose, adjust it by turning nut *A:*

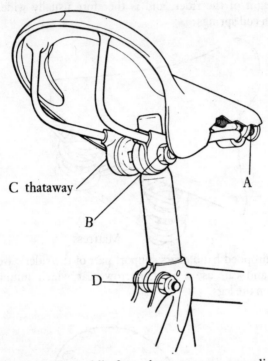

C thataway

B

A

D

To remove the saddle from the seat post, or to adjust its position backward, forward, or to tilt it, loosen nuts *B* and *C*. This applies also to mattress saddles. For proper saddle position refer to Fitting, pp. 45–47.

To raise or lower the saddle, loosen the binder bolt D.

Be sure to use a wrench which fits the nut exactly. It has to be tight, and the wrong tool can tear up the nut.

Only leather saddles need special care. A new leather saddle should be thoroughly saturated with neatsfoot oil from *underneath.*

Then, depending on how much you ride and how much you sweat, the saddle should be cleaned periodically with saddle soap and lightly dressed with neatsfoot oil. The idea is to keep the leather clean, nourished, and comfortably pliable. Once a year should be enough. You can avoid this bother by using a plastic saddle, but in warm weather you will slide about in your own sweat.

Trouble-shooting

Seat tilts or swivels unnecessarily. Tighten binding bolt nuts *B* and *C* (see opposite page).

If the seat bottoms harshly on bumps and you have a mattress type saddle – too bad. If you have a racing saddle, tighten nut *A*.

The seat post sinks slowly into the frame while you ride. This can be a real stinker. First see if the seat post is the correct diameter by checking that the lips of the seat tube do not meet at the binder bolt:

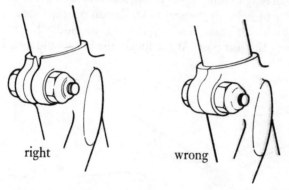

right   wrong

If the post is the right size and is greasy, try cleaning it and the inside of the seat tube thoroughly. On no account try the use of shims or abrasive material like emery paper between the seat tube and the seat post. The chances are excellent that some of the material will fall down the seat tube and get into the bottom bracket, where it will make mincemeat of your crankset bearings (thought seats were simple, hah?). The only sure-fire solution is to install a thin bolt through the seat post and seat tube at point *P*:

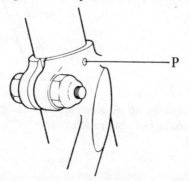

P

To do this you need a drill, hand or electric, a bolt, nut, and washer, and a drill bit. *Do all drilling with the bike upside down so that shavings do not fall down the seat tube into the bottom bracket.* If you are having a shop do the job make sure that they do this. Position seat at desired height. Make an initial dent with a center punch or with a hammer and sharp nail at point *P*. Then put a couple of drops of oil on the end of the drill bit and drill through. Go slowly to avoid heat build-up. Use single-speed electric drills in short bursts. You will want more than one saddle height position. To do this, loosen the binder bolt and rotate the seat post one eighth of a turn at the same time that you raise or lower it a little bit. Now use the already existing holes in the seat tube as a guide for drilling a new set of holes in the seat post. Repeat 3 or 4 times. The idea is to be able to make fine adjustments in saddle height without weakening the seat post. At the finish, the job should look like this:

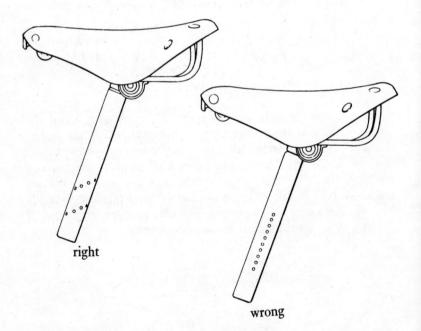

right

wrong

Be sure to clean up all shavings and filings so that they do not fall down into the bottom bracket.

Handlebars

Adjustments

To change handlebar position loosen binder bolt *A* on stem and reset bars:

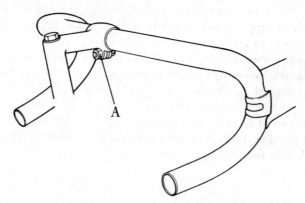

Height adjustments are made with the *stem* (p. 145).

Taping: I prefer non-adhesive plastic tape. Adhesive tapes gum everything up with a sticky residue which ultimately leaks out all over everything and especially your hands. Cloth tape feels good but gets dirty quickly and is hard to clean.

Be sure that the brakes are in the position you want. Start about 2″ from the stem. Use a small piece of scotch tape to hold down the end of the tape where you start. Work directly from the roll to minimize confusion, and maintain a continuous light tension as you apply the tape. First take a couple of turns at the starting point and then start down the bar, overlapping $\frac{1}{2}$ to $\frac{1}{3}$ of the tape. At the bends you will have to overlap more on the inside than the outside. For a neat job, loosen the brake lever mount (see p. 128), tape underneath, and retighten:

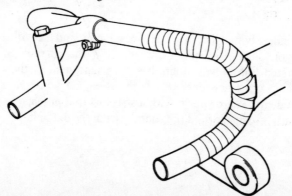

When you reach the end of the bar leave an extra 2–3″ of tape. Fold this over and push it inside the handlebar:

Finish off with a bar plug (bike stores) to hold tape securely. In a pinch this can be a cork or similar object. Use something — if you spill, an open bar end can make a hole in you.

Trouble-shooting

◎ Bar spins around on stem: tighten binder bolt *A*:

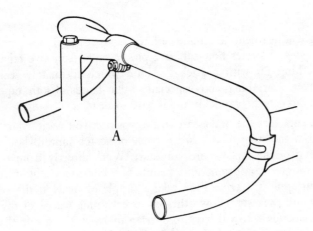

A

If binder bolt spins uselessly remove it and see if the little protrusion on it has been worn off, or if the corresponding slot on the stem into which it fits has been damaged. If the problem is the bolt, get a new one. If it is the stem, get a proper bolt with a hex nut that you can grip with a wrench. In a pinch, you can use pliers or vise-grips to hold the round part of the old bolt.

If binder bolt is in working order check and see that the lips of the stem do not meet:

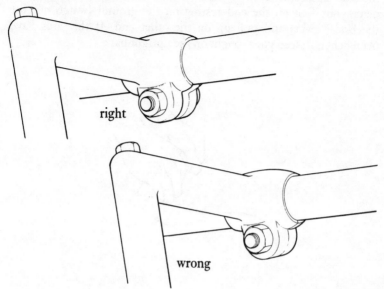

If they do, new bars (expensive) or a shim (cheap). Shimming: find a small piece of flat metal slightly longer than the width of the stem lips. Something that won't rust, like aluminum, is preferable (hardware stores, machine shop litter, junk lying around), but part of a tin can or a finishing nail will do. Remove binder bolt. Using a screwdriver, prise apart the lips of the stem:

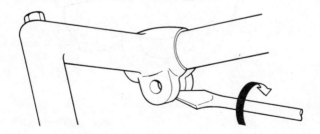

Slip the shim into the gap between the handlebar and the stem, and reinstall binder bolt.

◉ Bent bars: steel ones are hard to bend, alloy a lot easier. Lay
the bike on its side. If the ends of the handlebars have been bent in,
place your foot on the end resting on the ground (watch out for
the brake lever) and pull up on the other end. If the ends have
been bent out, lean your weight on the upright bar:

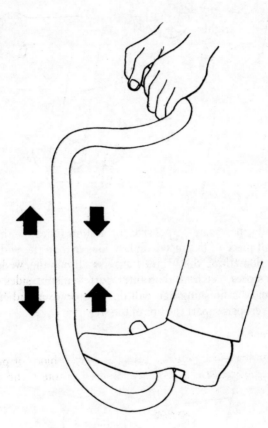

Stem

How It Works

The stem is a tube which holds the handlebar in position, and fits down inside the headset. The tube is split at the end, and down its length runs a bolt, called an expander bolt, which is attached to a wedge nut (A):

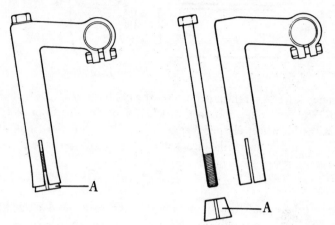

When the expander bolt is tightened, it draws the wedge nut into the tube, and this in turn forces apart the split sides of the stem, pressing them against the sides of the headset and holding everything in place.

Adjust or Remove

Undo expander bolt two turns. Using a wooden block or piece of cardboard held against the expander bolt to protect the finish, tap it with a hammer or heavy object:

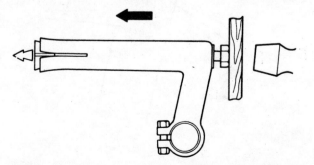

Repeat as necessary to get stem loose. Adjust height or remove. If you remove altogether and reassemble take note: some wedge nuts have a dog guide which must fit into a corresponding slot on the stem:

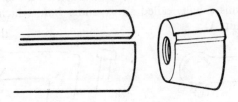

Keep at least $2\frac{1}{2}''$ of the stem tube in the headset.

Retighten expander bolt so that when you stand in front of the bike with the wheel clasped between your legs you can twist the handlebar and stem in the headset. This way, if you take a spill the bars will give instead of bending or breaking.

Trouble-shooting

◎ Stem is loose and expander bolt comes out freely: wedge nut has come off. Take out stem, turn bike upside down, and shake wedge nut out. Reassemble.

◎ Stem is frozen in place and expander bolt spins uselessly: threads on wedge nut have stripped (1), or expander bolt has snapped (2).

(1) Separate expander bolt from wedge nut by grasping it with pliers or vise-grips and maintaining a continuous upward pressure while twisting it. If it is obstinate, help it along by wedging a screwdriver between the expander bolt head and the stem:

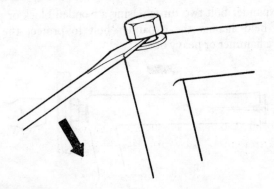

Once the expander bolt is free of wedge nut leave it inside the stem.

(2) Remove top half of snapped expander bolt. Find a rod or bolt which will fit inside stem and touch wedge nut while still protruding an inch or two above the stem.

(1) and (2): Use a hammer to lightly tap the expander bolt or rod, working the end inside the stem around the edges of the wedge nut:

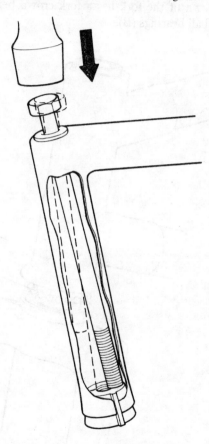

Work firmly but gently; too hard a blow will jam the whole thing. When stem comes loose, turn bike upside down and shake out wedge nut.

◎ Stem tube cracked. Replace it.

Headset

How It Works

The headset connects the front forks to the head tube of the bicycle frame and, through the stem, to the handlebars. The fork is held solidly to the bicycle but allowed to turn freely by using ball bearing sets at the top and bottom of the head tube. Starting at the bottom, the crown of the fork has a fork crown bearing race (A), then come the ball bearings (B),

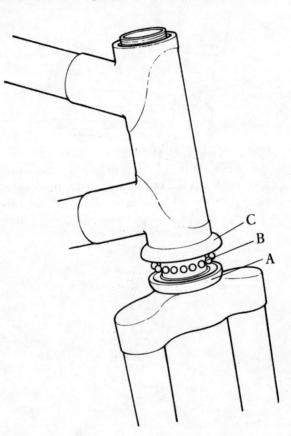

and next is the bottom set race (C), screwed or force-fitted into the head tube.

Put together, it looks like this:

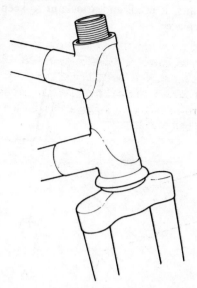

To keep the forks inside the head tube and evenly positioned, a second set of races is used at the top of the head tube. There is a top set race, screwed or force-fitted into the head tube, more ball bearings, and what actually keeps the forks in position is the top race, which is threaded onto the fork tube:

top race ——

top set race ——

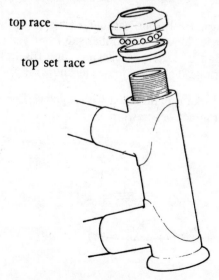

This is capped by a washer, the cable hanger and/or other accessory mounts, if used, and a locknut to keep the top threaded race exactly in place:

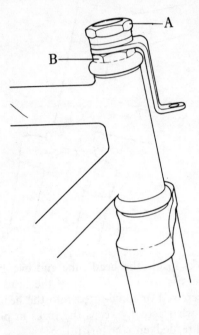

Routine Adjustments

Forks should turn freely but without excessive up and down play. A simple test for looseness is to lock the front brake and rock the bike forward and backward. A clicking noise from the headset indicates loose bearings. To adjust, loosen locknut *A* (above).

Sometimes this locknut is designed with notches. Loosen with a hammer and center punch or screwdriver:

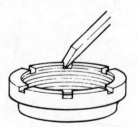

If you are using big wrenches or pliers be careful not to bend nuts or races.

Now turn down the threaded top race *B* handtight against the bearings, and then back it off one quarter turn.

Snug down locknut *A,* being careful to keep threaded top race *B* in position. Check play again.

Lubrication and Disassembly

The headset should be dismantled, cleaned, and regreased about once a year. Remove stem (p. 145) and front wheel (p. 158). Lay bike down on side with newspaper or white rag under the headset. This is to catch falling ball bearings. There are many different headsets, and no way for me to tell you how many are in yours. So don't lose any.

Undo and remove the locknut, washer, cable clamp (if you have one), and anything else necessary to get to the threaded top race. Secure the fork to the frame. You can do this with rubber bands, elastic carrier straps, shoelaces, etc., but the simplest way is to hold it with your hand. Be sure to do something, or what you do next will cause the fork to fall out along with a rain of ball bearings. Next: undo the threaded top race A :

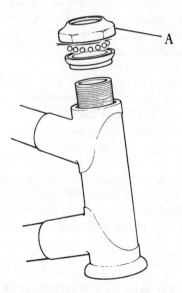

You will have loose ball bearings and are to follow instructions for (1), or bearings in a clip in which case follow (2).

(1) A few may stick to the threaded race, a few may fall on the newspaper, and most will probably stay in the top set race. Get them all together, count them, and put bearings and race into a box or jar. Next: make sure head tube is positioned over newspaper or rag. Slowly draw out fork tube. Ball bearings will fall out. Get and count them, including any that are still stuck to the bottom set race, the fork tube, or whatever, and put them in a jar.

(2) Clipped bearings: Lucky you. Remove clip, noting carefully which side goes down against the top set race, and put in a jar or box. Now draw out fork tube and lift out clip for bottom race.

Further disassembly for routine lubrication is not necessary.

(1) & (2) Soak and clean thoroughly all parts in solvent. Use a rag to clean out the top and bottom set races, and the fork crown race. Ball bearings should be smooth and unpitted. Clipped bearings should be securely in place. Races should be evenly colored all the way around where the balls run. Place them on a glass surface to see if they are bent or warped. Replace any defective parts.

Reassembly: pack fresh grease in the top and bottom set races. Just fill the grooves; excessive grease will attract dirt.

(1) Push ball bearings into grease on bottom set race. Grease will hold them in place.

(2) Put some grease inside the clip. Slip it down over the fork tube to rest on the fork crown race.

(1) & (2) Carefully insert fork tube into head tube. Keeping it snug against the bearings, check that it turns freely. Hang onto fork so that it does not fall back out.

(1) Stick ball bearings into grease of top set race.

(2) Grease and slip on clipped bearings.

(1) & (2) Screw down top threaded race. These threads are fine, so do it carefully (see General Notes, p. 104, for best technique). Set it hand tight, and then back it off one quarter turn. Pile on washer, cable anchor mount, etc., and locknut. Be careful to keep threaded top race in position when tightening locknut. Check for play.

Complete Disassembly

If the bike has been in a smash-up or if rust has got to the bearings, it may be necessary to do a complete disassembly.

Take fork and ball bearings out as per for lubrication. Remove crown fork race from fork. If it is stuck, pry it up *gently* with a screwdriver, working around the edges a little at a time. Be careful, it is easy to bend:

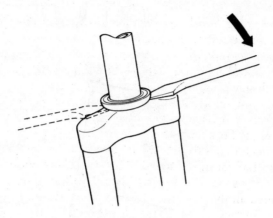

Remove top and bottom set races. You may possibly have threaded set races, in which case simply unscrew them. For force set races, insert a large screwdriver, piece of pipe, or stiff rod into the head tube and tap around the edges of the race:

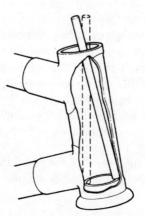

Clean all parts with solvent. Test races for uniformity by seeing if they lie flat on glass or other smooth surface.

Reassembly: screw in threaded set races. For force set races use a wooden block (to avoid denting or bending the race) and hammer:

Make sure that it is seated fully into the frame. Use a wooden block also on the fork crown race if it is balky but be very delicate, and tap evenly all the way around the race.

Trouble-shooting

◎ Fork tube is extremely loose in the head tube. May just need adjustment (p .148), but if things have come to this pass I suggest dismantling and checking condition of parts.

Adjustment does not work: top threaded race or fork is stripped. Dismantle and see. It is unlikely that this is the result of excessive tightening, and likely that the top threaded race was screwed down off center. When you have your new parts review General Notes, Threading p. 104, before starting.

◎ Fork binds or catches, or makes grating and rasping noises when you turn handlebars. Adjust as per p. 150 . No go? Something is broken or bent, completely worn out, or there are too many or too few ball bearings. Review the possibilities. Has fork or headset been whacked severely lately? A couple of months ago? Did you or someone else service the headset and lose a bearing or two, or place too many in one race and not enough in the other? Or perhaps the bike is simply ancient, and needs new races? In any case, disassemble (p.151), clean, and check all parts. Are bearings evenly distributed (ask your bike shop how many should be in your headset), and free of dents, cracks, and pitting? Do races lie flat on a glass surface? Replace defective parts and reassemble. If you can find nothing wrong take the parts down to your bike shop and see what they say.

Forks

How They Work

The fork holds the front wheel in place and allows the bike to be steered. The fork arms are curved, giving the axle dropouts rake or trail from a line drawn through the fork tube:

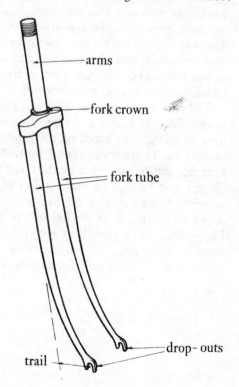

arms

fork crown

fork tube

trail

drop-outs

This rake or trail has two purposes: it makes the bike handle better, and it helps the bike to absorb bumps and other road shocks. The amount of trail varies as according to the purpose of the bike. Touring bikes have a slightly longer trail for a softer, more comfortable ride. Racing and track machines have a shorter trail for greater efficiency in transmitting rider effort to the wheels. Additionally, the forks may be solid or tubular, the latter lighter and more flexible.

Lubrication and Dismantling

Covered under Headset, p 151.

Trouble-shooting

◉ All problems with turning, grating noises, etc. are covered under Headset, pp 148-154

◉ Bent forks: replace them. Bending fatigues metal and makes it weak. The weakness does not show. What happens is that the fork suddenly gives up while you are tearing along at 30 m.p.h. This does not happen very often, but once is enough. Bicycle shops do have special tools for straightening bent forks and if the bend in yours is slight, you may want to try it. Be aware that you are taking a calculated risk, however small.

Tests for bent forks: the bike will ride funny. If forks are bent to one side, the bike will always want to turn to the left or right. Test by taking your hands off the handlebars. Any decently set — up bike can be ridden hands off for miles. Forks which have been bent in, usually through a head-on collision, make the bike's ride choppy and harsh, and make it feel like it wants to dive in the corners. A sure sign of bent-in forks is wrinkled paint on the upper fork arms, or at the join of the fork tube and fork crown. Forks which have been bent out (rare) manifest themselves in a sloppy, mushy ride, and curious, long arcing turns. Again, there will probably be paint wrinkles at the bend point.

4. Wheels

Contents/Index

Wheel Removal

Wheels need to be removed often, for a variety of reasons, and sometimes on the road. So you can and will do this with a free-standing bike, but it is much easier if it is hung up. Most 3-speeds and some 10-speeds can simply be turned upside down on handlebars and seat, as long as cables or shift selectors are not damaged. Bikes with caliper brakes in proper adjustment should require some slacking of the brakes (see pp. 110-11) so that the tire will pass between the brake shoes.

Front wheel, any bike

Wheel will be held to fork by hex nuts, wing nuts, or a quick-release lever:

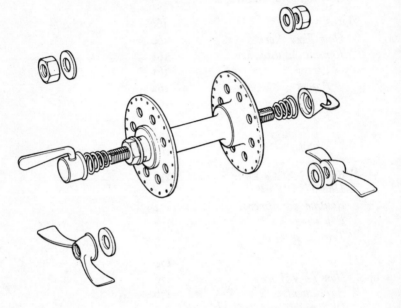

For nuts, undo both simultaneously (counter-clockwise) and unwind a turn or two. Levers, flip it. Remove wheel. Note washers go outside fork drop-outs.

Rear wheel

10-*speed bikes:*

Run chain to smallest sprocket. Undo nuts or lever as for front wheel, and push wheel down and out. If you have a free hand hold back the derailleur so that the freewheel clears it easily, otherwise just gently wiggle it by.

3-*speed bikes:*

Shift to 3rd gear. Disconnect shift cable at rear hub by undoing locknut A and unscrewing adjustor sleeve B from pole:

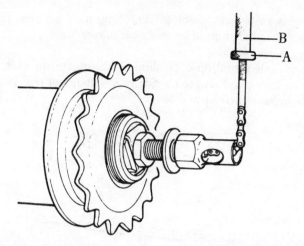

Undo nuts simultaneously (counter-clockwise). Remove wheel, and note washers are outside drop-outs.

Single-speed coaster-brake bikes:

Disconnect coaster-brake bracket from bike frame (metal arm at left end of rear axle), undo nuts (counter-clockwise), and remove wheel.

Replacing Wheels

Front, any bike

Axle with nuts: back off nuts a few turns and slip axle onto drop-outs. Washers go outside drop-outs. Set nuts finger tight and check that rim is centered between fork arms before snugging them down. Re-set caliper brakes if you have them.

Levers: Slip axle onto drop-outs with lever on left side of bike. If this is difficult, hold knurled cone with one hand and unwind lever a couple of turns with the other. Slip axle on drop-outs and wind lever down just short of finger tight. Check that wheel rim is centered between fork arms, and close lever so that it points upwards and backwards. It should be firmly shut but not hysterically so. Re-set caliper brakes.

Rear wheels

10-speed bikes:

Work axle into drop-outs, slipping chain over smallest sprocket on freewheel. Set nuts or lever for light tension. Pull wheel toward rear of bike until right end of axle hits the back of the drop-out.

Use this as a pivot point to center the rim between the chain stays, and tighten nuts or lever. Re-set caliper brake.

3- and 1-speed bikes:

Work axle into drop-outs, slipping chain over sprocket. Lightly tighten nuts (washers are outside drop-outs), and pull back wheel so chain has ½" play up and down:

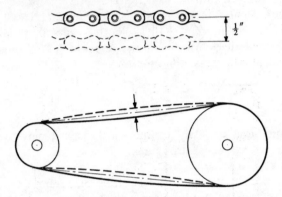

Center rim between chain stays and tighten down nuts. Check chain tension. 1-speed bikes, reconnect coaster brake bracket to frame. 3-speed bikes, with gear selector in 3rd, reconnect barrel sleeve to hub gear chain, and set locknut with cable slightly slack. Test gears and adjust if necessary (pp.203-4). Re-set caliper brake.

Tires

How They Work

Any pneumatic tire works by supporting a casing, the part touching the road, with an inside tube which is filled with air like a balloon. With tubular tires the tube is fully encased by the casing; with clincher tires the tube is held in place by a combination of two wire beads which run around the outside edges of the tire, and the rim sides:

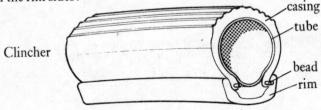

Clincher

casing
tube
bead
rim

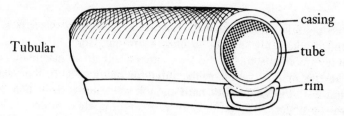

Tubular

casing

tube

rim

Air is pumped into the tube through a valve which comes in two types. Almost all clincher tires have Schraeder valves, the kind typically found on cars. A few clinchers and all tubulars have 'Presta' type valves, which require either a bicycle pump, or a special adaptor for gas station air pumps:

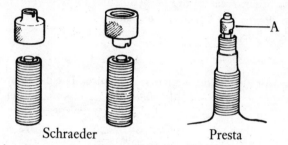

A

Schraeder   Presta

'Presta' valves need to have the locknut A undone in order to be pumped up.

Tire Selection

There are tires for nearly every purpose and condition: rain, mud, racing, touring, and carrying heavy loads. In tubulars heavy-duty 15-16 ounce tires are about the only practical choice for touring and general use. Racers use lighter tires which run 7 to 11 ounces. In clincher tires I suggest you explain your needs to a shop and try their recommendation.

Generally, 3-speeds are fitted with an all-purpose coarse – thread heavy-duty tire, and 10-speeds with a lighter road pattern tire. Better tires cost only a little more and are worth it in the long run.

Routine Adjustments

Tire pressure

Use your own tire pressure gauge (bike shops). Gas station gauges are unreliable. When filling your tires at a gas station do it yourself. The proper pressure for your tire may be as high as

100 pounds per square inch, but the total volume of air is small, and it takes only seconds to blow a tire out. Some air pumps take a few moments to fill the tire; others will do it instantaneously. Jab the air hose down on the valve for just a second, then release and test. Tires should be hard enough so you can barely dent them with a finger, and bulge only very slightly when ridden. Consult chart below for proper pressure.

Bicycle pump and Schraeder valve: draw hose fitting out of pump handle and fit to pump and valve. Check connections periodically and as you pump. 'Presta' valve: undo valve locknut, push pump on valve, hold firmly to tire with one hand, and pump with the other. Keep pump perpendicular to valve. Disengage with a sharp downward knock of the hand; wiggling will lose air and possibly bend valve.

Recommended Pressures

Note: for heavier loads increase pressure. The difference between pressure for a 125 pound rider and 200 pound rider is about 15 to 20 pounds per square inch.

Tubular 27" – Rear, 85 to 100; front, 75–90.

Clincher 27" – 75 to 90

Clincher 26" X 1¼" – 45 to 60.

X 1½" – 40 to 55.

X 1⅜" – 40 to 55.

X 1¾" – 35 to 45.

24" – 35 to 45.

20" – 45 to 50.

18" – 35 to 45.

16" – 30 to 40.

12" – 30 to 40.

Check tire pressure often. Tubular tires "breathe" air through the sides and need filling frequently. Hot weather in the 80's and up may require that you bleed some air from the tire to avoid over-inflation and a possible blow-out.

Riding

Most tire problems are the result of picked-up debris working into the casing as you ride. Going over rocks, through pot-holes, and on and off curbs will cause ruptures. Cultivate an eye for these hazards, and if you are forced to go through a patch of broken glass, for example, check and see that the tire has not picked any up. A useful gadget for tubular tires is a nail-catcher (bike shops) which rides lightly over the tire and brushes off particles before they can cause damage:

Keep oil away from tires. It rots rubber. Grease, do not oil bicycle pumps. Oiled bicycle pumps can vaporize and blow oil inside the tube. Check cement on tubulars about once a week.

Care and Storage

Keep clincher spares in a dry place. Tubular spares should be carried folded so the tread is on the outside and not folded back on itself .Under the seat is a dandy place. Secure with straps or rubber bands:

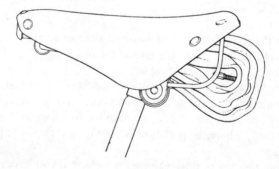

Every two weeks or so inflate a folded spare and let it stand for a while. Refold in the opposite direction.

Flats

Flats take the form of violent blow outs (rare), or punctures (common) which leak air with varying degrees of speed. Blow outs are usually terminal, doing so much damage that the tube and sometimes the tire must be replaced. Punctures which are not gaping wounds can be repaired. There is debate as to proper policy for this and some bike shops maintain that any patching is "temporary" and prefer to install a new tube. I suggest that you patch newish tubes and throw out older ones.

Clincher tires

You will need a tube patch kit containing patches, glue, an abrasive surface, tire irons (the kind which hook onto spokes are handiest), and chalk.

First check valve by inflating tire slightly and placing a drop of spit on the end of the valve stem. A leaky valve will bubble or spit back. Tighten valve if necessary with valve cap or suitable part of pressure gauge:

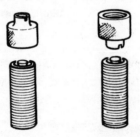

Hooray if the problem was a loose or defective valve. If not, spin the wheel and look for an obvious cause like a nail or piece of glass. Yes? Dig it out and mark the spot.

What you do next depends on circumstances. It is easier to work on a puncture with the wheel off the bike (see p. 157). However, you may not have the tools to accomplish this feat, or perhaps you know exactly where the puncture is. At any rate, the basic procedure is the same.

Deflate tire and remove valve stem locknut if you have one. Work the tire back and forth with your hands to get the bead free of the rim. If the tire is a loose fit on the rim you may be able to get it off with your hands. This is best, because tire irons may pinch the tube and cause additional punctures. To do this make sure that the bead is free of the rim all the way around. Take a healthy grip on the tire with both hands and pull it up and off-center so that one bead comes over the rim:

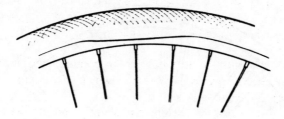

Then go around the rim working the bead completely off.

You will probably need to use tire irons. Use tire irons, not screwdrivers, as these are likely to cut the tube. Free bead from rim. Insert tire iron under bead, being careful not to pinch the tube, and lever it over the side:

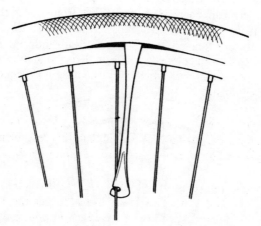

Insert second iron 2″ or 3″ away from first iron, and past where bead is over side of rim. Lever iron. For most tires this will do the job. No? A third iron. If this doesn't work, use the now free 2nd iron for a fourth attempt:

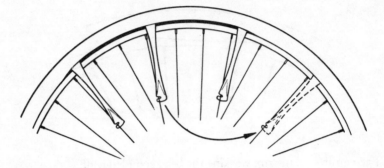

and repeat process as often as necessary.

If you don't have tire irons which hook onto the spokes, then you will need to use elbows, knees, etc. to hold down the irons as you work away. Be careful not to inadvertently crush a spoke, and keep your face away in case something slips and tire irons start jumping about.

If you have only two tire irons and need a third, scrounge something up. In the country a flat rock or a stick. In the city a pencil, a beer can opener, or something from the garbage. Look around. At the hour there will be *something*. Prise up bead with a tire iron. Insert foraged tool between bead and rim and wiggle iron out:

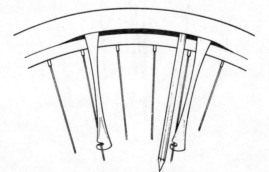

Use tire irons to make two prises on either side of foraged tool.

One bead is off rim. Push valve stem up into tire, and remove tube. Use chalk or eidetic memory to make note of which way tube was in the tire. Inflate tube and rotate it past your ear. If you can locate the puncture through the hiss of escaping air mark it with chalk. No? Immerse tube in water and look for escaping air bubbles. Dry tube with a rag while holding finger over puncture, then mark with chalk.

Take sandpaper or metal abrader supplied with patch kit and rough up the area around the puncture. Spread a layer of cement over this area and let dry tacky. Peel the paper backing off a patch without touching the surface thus exposed, and press it firmly on the puncture. Hold for a moment next to tire with valve stem alongside valve hole and note where puncture occurred. Set tube aside to dry.

If puncture was on inside of tube probably a protruding spoke caused it:

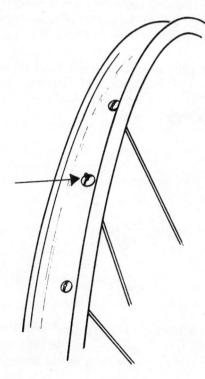

File the spoke flush with the rim. Check other spokes.

If the puncture was on the outside of the tube find what caused it by rubbing your fingers around inside the casing. Check the rest of the casing for embedded particles, and for ruptures or breaks:

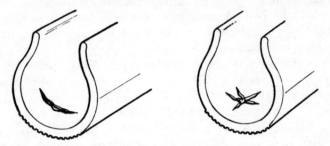

Replace the tire at the first opportunity if it has these.

To install the tube, first inflate it slightly to prevent it from folding and pinching itself. Push the part of the tube with the valve stem into the tire, and the valve stem through its hole on the rim. Fit valve stem locknut loosely. Stuff rest of tube into tire being careful not to pinch or tear it. Check that valve stem is still straight.

Push valve stem partway out, and slip bead of tire at that point back over the rim. It is important that you hold the base of the valve stem clear of the rim as you do this, or the bead may catch on it, creating a bulge in the tire:

Work around the rim replacing the bead and always taking care not to pinch the tube. Ideally you can do the entire job with your hands. Check that the valve stem is still straight. The last bit will be hard. Just keep working at it with your thumbs, first from one side, then from the other. When about 2″ of bead remains give it the grand mal effort. Don't wonder if it will go over; decide that it will. If you have to use a tire iron, be very careful not to pinch the tube.

Tubular tires

You will need:
Patches
Needle
Thread
Rubber cement
Sandpaper
Talcum powder
Chalk
Screwdriver
Sharp knife or razor blade

Remove wheel (p. 157). Deflate tire completely by opening locknut A on valve and holding down:

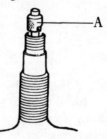

Remove tire from rim with your hands. Inflate and immerse in water a little at a time. Do not be misled by air bubbles coming out by the valve. Since the tire is sewn, the valve hole and puncture hole are the only places air can escape. Hold finger over puncture when located, dry tire, and mark puncture with chalk.

With a screwdriver or similar implement pry away about 5″ to 6″ of the tape on the inner side of the tire at the puncture area:

Next cut stitching about 2″ to either side of puncture. Make only two cuts to avoid numerous bits and pieces of thread, and cut upwards to miss tire:

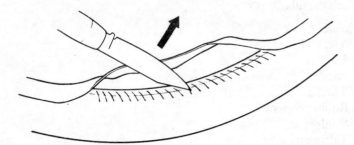

Gently remove tube and locate leak. A mixture of soap and water will pin-point elusive ones. Dry tube if wet. Abrade area around puncture with sandpaper. Apply cement and let dry. Peel protective paper from patch without touching surface thus exposed and apply to puncture. Dust with talc to prevent tube from sticking to casing. Get whatever caused puncture out of casing. Insert tube, inflate, and check for leaks. Do this carefully. You are going to be mad if you get it all back together only to discover it still leaks.

Thread the needle and knot the two loose ends of thread. In a pinch 12 pound linen thread or silk fishing line will do. Using the old holes, start with an overlap of about $\frac{1}{2}″$, i.e. $\frac{1}{2}″$ past where thread was cut. Pinch the sides of the casing between thumb and forefinger to keep the tube out of the way:

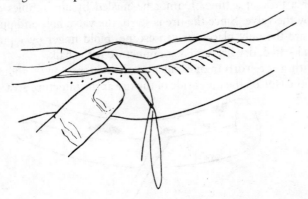

Pull stitches firm, but not so tight as to cut casing. Finish with a ½" overlap into original stitching. Layer cement on casing and inside of peeled-away tape and keep apart until dry. Position carefully and press together firmly.

Mounting a tubular

New rims and tires: inflate tire, deflate, place on rim (see below), inflate, deflate, remove.

Repaired tires and/or old rims: clean off old cement from rim with shellac thinner or solvent (bike stores).

There are two methods of mounting a tubular.

(1) Slow but sure. Deflate tire. Insert valve. Stand rim on soft surface with valve stem up, and working from above, work tire down over rim:

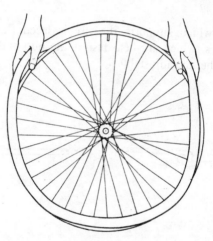

Be careful to distribute tire evenly around rim. Finish by grabbing with both hands and getting the last bit over by main force:

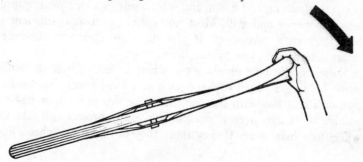

Check again that tire is evenly distributed and centered on rim. Roll back a portion of the tire and brush glue on rim and lining. Repeat all the way around and from both sides. Check again for evenness. Inflate hard. Allow half a day to dry before using or tire may creep (bunch up in spots) or simply come off the rim in a corner.

(2) Fast method. Apply glue to rim and tire and allow to dry tacky. Wear old clothes and assemble as above.

Road repairs: use the old cement on the rim and don't lean hard into corners going home. Double-sided rim tape (bike stores) is very handy.

Rims and Spokes

How They Work

The rim which supports the tire is laced (held) in position by the spokes, which are held fast at the hub and screw into the rim, so that they are adjustable:

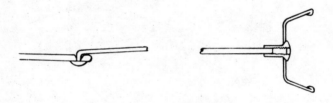

Adjustments

The tension on the spokes relative to each other determines both the strength and position of the rim. Positioning the rim correctly, both up and down, and side to side, is a long job requiring lots of patience and skill. Most times it is much more efficient to leave this to a bike shop. If you have no alternative however, or are determined to go it alone, here's how:

Hang up the bike or place the wheel in a jig. Spin the wheel while holding a pencil or some-such at a fixed point like the fork arm or a seat stay with the point near the rim to see how bad the wobble is. If it is over $\frac{1}{2}''$ pack up the entire project and take the wheel to a bike store. If they think they can save the wheel, fine, otherwise get a new wheel.

With a less than ½″ wobble: deflate tire. If job looks to be major, it will be easier if you just remove the tire altogether. Pluck the spokes with your fingers – they should all "ping" – and tighten any that are slack so that they all have an even tension. Spokes are tightened by turning *counter- clockwise*. If in the course of doing this you find spokes with frozen nipples (the part which holds the spoke to the rim) they must be replaced (see below). If it is more than 3 or 4 spokes I once again suggest resorting to your friendly bike shop.

Hold a chalk or pencil at the *outer edge* of the rim while you spin the wheel so that the high spots are marked. Working one half to 1 turn at a time, tighten the spokes at the chalk mark (*counter-clockwise*) and loosen them opposite the chalk mark. Continue until wheel is round.

Hold pencil or chalk at *side* of rim so that side to side wobbles are marked. Working ½ to 1 turn at a time, and in groups of 4 to 6 spokes, tighten up the spokes opposite the chalk mark and loosen the ones next to it:

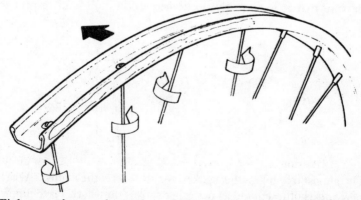

Tighten or loosen the spokes which are in the center of the chalk marks a little more than the ones at the edges of the marks. When you have finally succeeded, or compromised, run your finger around the rim and check for protruding spoke ends. File protruders down.

Replacing Spokes

Remove tire (p. 157). If you are dealing with spokes on a

freewheel-equipped rear wheel that go to the freewheel side of the hub the freewheel will have to be removed (p. 199). Take broken spokes out of hub and rim. Get replacements which are exactly the same; many different kinds are available.

New spokes should go into hub so that head is on opposite side of hub from adjoining spokes and spoke is pointed in opposite direction:

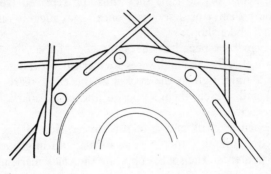

Be sure that it is correctly positioned in the hub with respect to the bevels:

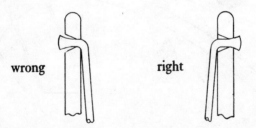

On almost all bikes the spokes touch where they cross. Weave new spokes through old as per other spokes on wheel. Place nipples on spokes and tighten. True wheel (see above), file down any protruding spokes which might puncture the tube, and remount tire.

Trouble-shooting

◎ For side-to-side wobbles and elliptical wheels see p. 172.
◎ For bulges in the rim caused by piling into curbs, stones, etc.: you will need vise-grips, channel-lock pliers, or a C-clamp. If

bulge is equal on both sides of rim place implement over bulge and squeeze *gently* until the rim is even again:

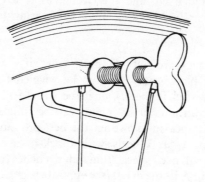

If the bulge is on one side of the rim, distribute the pinching force of your implement on the non-bulge side with a block of wood or some such:

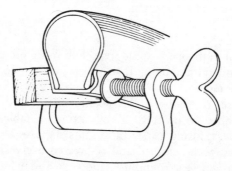

Fixing bulges almost invariably leaves a slight dimple because the metal itself was stretched, but the wheel will probably be usable.

Hubs

We are talking here about any front wheel hub or freewheel equipped rear wheels. Multi-speed hubs are too complicated to service.

How They Work

A hub consists of an axle, two sets of bearings, and a casing. The axle is held fixed, and the casing, to which the spokes are attached, spins around it riding on the ball bearings(see opposite).

Adjustments

Wheel bearings are out of adjustment if, with the axle held firmly in place, the wheel can be wiggled from side to side (usually with a clicking noise), or if the wheel will not turn easily. Wheels held with nuts or lever nuts can be adjusted while on the bike. Generally speaking however, the best procedure is to remove the wheel (p. 157). Wheels with quick-release hubs must be removed. You will need special thin hub wrenches (bike stores).

Undo locknut A from cone B (see opposite page).

Holding axle or axle housing (quick-releases) still with wrench at locknut C (ten-speed rear wheels: if you can't get at it with a wrench use vise-grips or pliers), screw cone B fully home and then back off one quarter turn. Lock in place with locknut A. Test for side to side play. Wheel should spin freely, and on good hubs the weight of the tire valve will pull the wheel around so that the valve rests in the six o'clock position.

Lubrication

Any front hub or 10-speed rear hub with oil clips or caps: $\frac{1}{2}$ teaspoonful oil a month. If a grease fitting, one or two shots of grease per month.

Multi-speed rear hubs: 1 tablespoonful oil.

Coaster brake rear hubs: if oil fitting, 2 tablespoonfuls per month; if grease fitting, two or three shots of grease.

Hubs need to be cleaned and re-greased every six months for bikes in constant year-round use, and once a year for bikes retired for the winter or used only moderately. This requires disassembly.

Disassembly and Replacement

Remove wheel from bike (p. 157). Ten-speed rear wheels, remove freewheel (pp.199-200). Lay wheel down on rags or newspaper to catch ball bearings. Undo locknut A from cone B and remove both while holding on to axle at C.

Remove dust cover D. To do this it may be necessary to let the

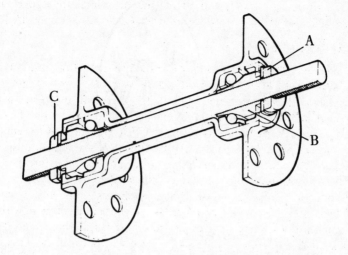

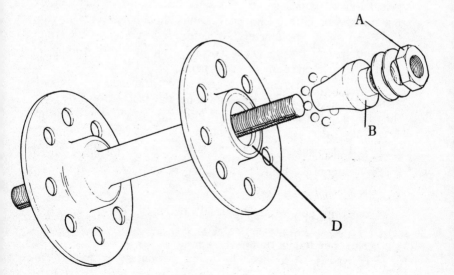

axle drop in just a little way so you can pry the dust cover off with a screwdriver:

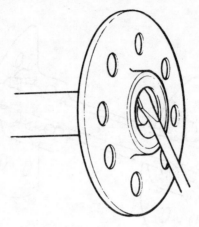

Prise out the loose or clipped ball bearings (or turn the wheel over and dump them out), count, and place in jar. Now slide axle all the way out and dump out remaining bearings. Garner and count. Undo remaining locknut and cone and remove from axle. Clean all parts in solvent. Examine bearings to see that they are not cracked or pitted. Clipped bearings should be secure in clip. Cups and cones should be even in color all around where bearings run and free of pitting. Text axle for straightness by rolling on glass surface. Replace any defective parts.

Reassembly: pack cups with grease. Not too much, excess will attract grit. Replace and lock one cone and locknut on axle. Slip dust cover on axle. Pack bearings into cup on one side of wheel. Gracefully insert axle and turn wheel over. Pack bearings into cup, replace dust cover, screw on cone and locknut, and adjust as per above.

Trouble-shooting

If something goes wrong it is usually because
   (1) the hub hasn't been serviced, or
   (2) a cone and locknut have come adrift.
In either case, if routine adjustment will not solve the problem, completely disassemble hub and replace broken or defective parts as per above.

5. Power Train

Contents/Index

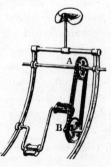

Pedals

How They Work

A pedal consists of a platform of metal or metal and rubber for the foot, an axle (called a spindle) which screws into the crank, and two sets of ball bearings on which the platform rides as it spins around the spindle.

Adjustment

If pedal can be wiggled back and forth on the spindle it needs tightening. Remove dustcap A (pry with a screwdriver if it is the wedge type):

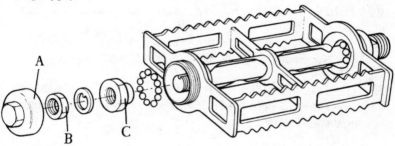

Undo locknut B from cone C. Screw cone C fully home and back off ¼ turn. Secure with locknut B. Check for play and that pedal spins easily. Replace dustcap A.

Lubrication and Disassembly

Pedals lead a hard, dissolute life and need cleaning and re-greasing every six months, more often if you ride a lot or favor wet weather. This requires disassembly. Remove pedals from crank. *Note:* right-hand pedal has a conventional right-hand thread and unscrews by turning counter-clockwise, but left-hand pedal has a left-hand thread and unscrews by turning *clockwise*. Work with pedal over newspaper or rag to catch ball bearings. Remove dustcover A (see illustration above). Undo and remove locknut B and cone C while holding platform and spindle together with hand. Get all bearings out of dust cover end and place in jar. Remove spindle and place all bearings from crank end in jar. Clean all parts in solvent. Check ball bearings for pitting, cracks, disorderly conduct; cups and cones for uneven wear, pitting; spindle for straightness.

Reassembly: pack grease into cups on platform. Pack ball bearings into cup on crank side of platform (grease will hold them in place), and slide on spindle. Pack bearings into dust cover side cup. Screw down cone C fully home and back off one-quarter-turn. Secure with locknut B. Check for play and that pedal spins easily. Replace dustcover.

Note: When replacing pedals on bike be sure that left-side pedal, stamped "L" on end of spindle shaft, goes to the left side. It screws on *counter-clockwise*. The right-hand pedal is stamped "R" (surprise!) and screws on *clockwise*.

Trouble-shooting

◎ Pedal is tight to crank but askew. Bent spindle. Replace immediately.

◎ Grinding noises, hard to turn pedal. Try routine adjustment as above. No? Something is probably broken. Disassemble as above and replace defective parts.

◎ Loose pedal. Check that it is tight to crank. Left pedal tightens *counter-clockwise*, right pedal tightens *clockwise*. No? Loose bearings. Adjust as per above.

Cranks

Cranks support the pedals and transmit pedaling power to the front sprocket(s). They are attached to a bottom bracket axle which rides on two sets of ball bearings inside the bottom bracket shell. There are three types of cranks: one-piece; cottered three-piece; and cotterless three-piece:

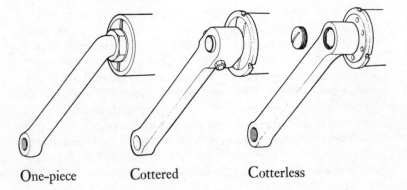

One-piece   Cottered   Cotterless

Since one-piece cranks include the bottom bracket axle, they are covered under Bottom Brackets. To test a cottered or cotterless crank for tightness, position the pedals equidistant from the ground. Press firmly on both pedals with hands and release. Rotate crankset one-half- turn and press pedals again. If something gives one of the cranks is loose.

Adjustment-Removal

Cottered Cranks

Support the crank with a block of wood which has a hole or V-notch into which the cotter pin A fits:

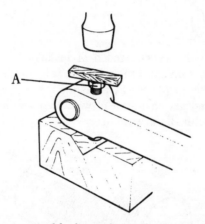

Be sure that the support block touches only the crank and is firmly in place. Otherwise what you do next will damage your bearings by driving the balls into the sides of the cup and scoring it (called Brinelling). Next: if you are tightening, give the head of the cotter pin A 2 or 3 moderate blows with a wooden mallet or hammer and wooden block combination. Then snug down nut firmly, but not with all your might or you will strip it. If you are removing, undo cotter pin 2 or 3 turns and then tap threaded end of cotter pin. Repeat if necessary. Be careful not to damage the threads as you will want to use the pin again. If you use a new pin and it does not fit, file down the flat side until it does.

Cotterless Cranks—

You will need a crank installer and extractor which fits your particular brand of crank. Cotterless cranks are made of an aluminum alloy called dural and must not be tightened with the same force as steel parts. To tighten or loosen first remove the dust cover A:

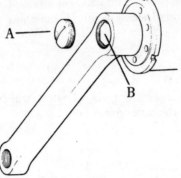

To tighten, apply socket wrench of installer to nut B and turn down, wiggling crank arm to make sure it is seated all the way. For new cranks retighten every 25 miles for the first 200 miles of use. To remove, first get chain out of way. Remove nut B. Back inner bolt A of extractor all the way out:

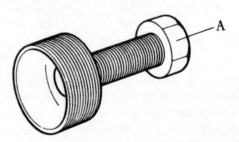

Screw extractor into crank, and then tighten down inner bolt A. *Do not do this with all of your might or you may strip the threads.* If the crank does not come loose with a firm tightening on the extractor bolt, give it 2 or 3 taps with a hammer, and tighten it one-eighth of a turn. Repeat until crank comes free. When replacing crank, be sure to wiggle it around a lot so that it is fully home before you give it the final tightening.

Trouble-shooting

◉ There is a "click" as you bring the pedal around on the

upstroke and then a momentary dead spot and another "click" as you push it down. It may be a loose pedal (p. 182), bottom bracket (p. 189), or crank. If it looks to be the crank, test and tighten if necessary as per above.

◎ Stripped holding bolt on a cotterless crank. Get a new bottom bracket axle. If this is impossible, a machine shop may be able to re-thread the axle to accept a larger bolt. Be sure that the head of the larger bolt is small enough so that you can still use an extractor.

◎ Stripped thread for the extractor on a cotterless crank. First ask your bike shop if they can solve the problem. No? You may be able to find a substitute tool which will do the job. I have one which looks like:

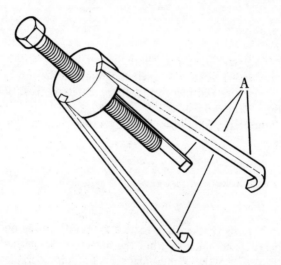

I have no idea what it is used for although I think it has something to do with plumbing. Anyway, the arms A will hook onto the crank or sprocket while the bolt passes against the bottom bracket axle.

If you can't find a substitute tool you and a machine shop may be able to manufacture a new extractor. It will be some trouble, but at upwards of $75 for fancy new cranks it is probably worth taking a stab at saving the old ones. Take your bike to a machine shop and explain that you want a steel plate or bar threaded in the center for an extractor bolt, and with holes drilled so that other bolts can be slid through and in turn be attached to metal plates which will hook behind the front sprocket:

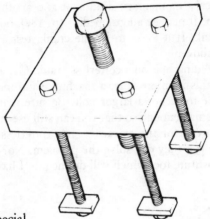

Backyard Special

If this Backyard Machine Shop Special Gizmo doesn't appeal to you, try jury-rigging your own conglomerate design of C-clamps, bolts, levers, bits and pieces and other materials. Just don't destroy your bike in the process.

◎ Bent crank. Should be fixed by a bike shop with a special tool for the job.

Bottom Bracket

How It Works

The bottom bracket axle (called a spindle) spins on two sets of ball bearings contained within the bottom bracket shell, and holds the cranks. On the Ashtabula type one-piece crankset, the two cranks and spindle are one unit. Three-piece cranksets (cottered and cotterless) consist of two cranks and a separate spindle. Although service techniques are fundamentally similar, we will discuss one-piece cranksets and spindles for three-piece cranksets separately.

Ashtabula one-piece crankset

Adjustment

If axle is hard to turn, or slips from side to side in bottom bracket shell, first remove chain (p. 193). Then loosen locknut A by turning it *clockwise:*

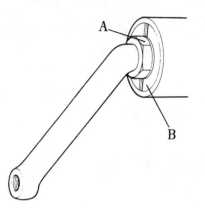

Use screwdriver in slot of cone B to turn it fully home (*counter-clockwise*), and then back it off one-eighth turn. Resecure locknut A (*counter- clockwise*), and check that cranks spin freely without side to side play.

Lubrication and Disassembly

Bottom bracket axles should be cleaned and re-greased once a year. This requires disassembly. Bearings for one-piece cranksets are held in clips so don't worry about losing them. Remove left pedal (*clockwise*) and chain from front sprocket (p. 193). Undo locknut A (*clockwise*), and unscrew cone B (*clockwise*) :

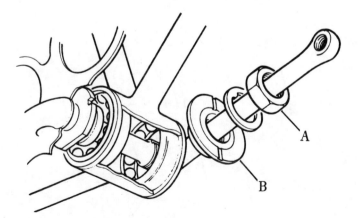

Remove ball bearing clip. Slide all parts off crank and place in a jar. Now move axle to right and tilt to slide whole unit through bottom bracket and out of frame. Take right side bearing clip off axle. Clean everything thoroughly with solvent. See that ball bearings are secure in clips and free from pitting or cracks; cups and cones are even in color where ball bearings run and free from pitting or scoring. If cups are deeply grooved replace. Remove with hammer and steel rod or screwdriver:

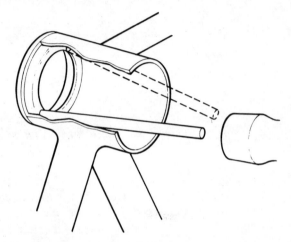

and make sure the new cups are well seated by tapping them in with a hammer and wooden block:

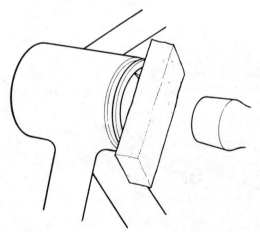

To reassemble: pack grease into bearing clips and cups. Slide one clip on axle with solid side against right cone. Gracefully insert crankset through bottom bracket shell from right side. Slide on ball bearing clips with balls in, solid side out. Screw on cone *(counter-clockwise)*, and turn it fully home, wiggling and spinning the crankset as you do this. Back off one-eighth turn and secure with locknut (tighten *counter-clockwise*). Check that crankset spins freely without side to side play. Replace pedal *(counter-clockwise)* and chain.

Three-piece Cranksets—

Adjustment

Bottom bracket axle (spindle) should be free from side to side play and spin freely. To adjust, first disconnect chain from front sprocket (p. 193).' Loosen notched lockring C on left side of bracket with a "C" wrench (bike stores) or hammer and screwdriver combination *(counter-clockwise)* :

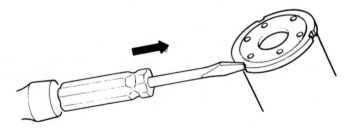

Then tighten *(clockwise)* adjustable cup D fully home with a screwdriver or center-punch inserted in hole or slot and *very light* hammer taps:

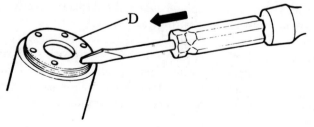

Back off one-eighth turn and secure with lockring C. Check that spindle spins freely and has no side to side play.

Lubrication and Disassembly

Bottom bracket assembly should be cleaned and re-greased once a year. This requires disassembly. Remove chain from front sprocket (p. 193) and cranks (p. 183). Lay bike right side down on newspaper or rags to catch loose ball bearings. Undo lockring C with "C" wrench or hammer and screwdriver combination and remove. Carefully holding axle in place against right side bearings, remove adjustable cup D:

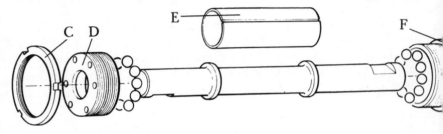

Lookout for the ball bearings! Some will fall out, others will stick to various parts. Get, count, and place in jar. Make sure you have them all. If your bearings are clipped, lucky you. Now pull spindle straight out. Garner all the right side ball bearings and jar 'em.

There may be a plastic tube (E, above) inside the bottom bracket shell. This is to prevent grit in the frame tubes from falling into the bearings. Take it out and clean it off. Clean out inside of bottom bracket shell with solvent. Examine the fixed cup F with a flashlight. If it is unpitted and wear is reasonably even, leave it alone. Otherwise unscrew and replace. Clean all other parts in solvent. See that ball bearings have no pits or cracks, and if clipped are secure in retainers; inside of adjustable cup and cones on spindle also have no pits and wear is even; spindle is straight. Replace defective parts.

Reassembly: pack cups with grease. If ball bearings are clipped, pack retainers. Replace plastic sleeve. Pack ball bearings into cups. Grease will hold in place. Clipped bearings go with solid side on cone (balls face out). Carefully insert spindle, long end to sprocket side of bottom bracket shell. Without jarring loose ball bearings fit on adjustable cup and screw home. Rotate spindle as you do this to make sure it goes in all the way. Back off one-eighth turn and secure with lockring. Be careful threading this on as it is easy to strip. Check that spindle spins easily with no side to side play. Replace cranks (p. 183) and chain (p. 195).

Trouble-shooting

◉ Tight or loose crankset, grinding noises. Try adjustment as above. No? Disassemble and replace defective parts as per above.

◉ "Click" on pedal upstroke followed by dead spot and second "click" on downstroke. Could be a loose spindle, but more probably a loose crank or pedal (p. 182).

Front Sprocket(s) (Chainwheel)

The front sprocket is the business with all the teeth attached to the right crank which pulls the chain around to deliver power to the rear wheel.

Adjustment

The only maintenance needed is to check periodically for bent or chipped teeth. Remove chain (p. 193). With a strong light behind the front sprocket, rotate it, looking from the side for chipped teeth, and from above or in front for bent teeth:

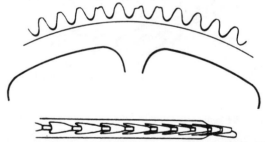

If teeth are chipped, replace sprocket (see below). If bent, take an adjustable wrench, snug it down over the bent tooth, and bend it back:

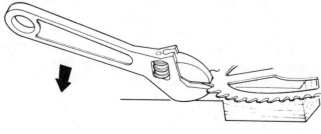

It helps a lot if you can brace the sprocket as you do this to avoid bending it.

Replacement

If it is necessary to replace your sprocket take a look at the chapter on gearing (pp 49-56). You might be interested in changing the number of gear teeth.

Ashtabula one-piece cranksets require replacing the whole unit (p. 187).

One-speed and most 3-speed bikes have a one-piece right crank and sprocket. To remove see p. 190.

Ten-speed bikes generally have a sprocket which is bolted to the right crank:

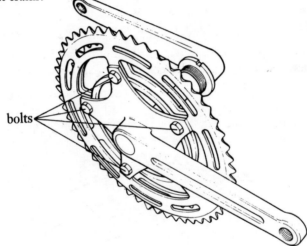

bolts◄

Simply undo the bolts (or allen screws) to remove sprocket.

Trouble-shooting

◉ There is a "clunk" every time you bring the front sprocket around. One possible cause is a bent tooth. Check by hanging bike up and slowly running sprocket. If chain suddenly jumps up where it meets the sprocket – bent tooth. Fix as above.

◉ Sprocket wobbles from side to side, hitting front derailleur cage or rubbing chainstays. If this is not due to incredibly loose bottom bracket bearings (p. 189), the sprocket is warped. Fixing is a job requiring both great delicacy and considerable force.

Techniques vary so much as according to the exact problem that I strongly suggest you leave it to a bike shop.

Chain

The chain is that innocent and simple looking business which transmits power to the rear gear(s). There are two kinds: one is used on non-derailleur bikes, is $\frac{1}{8}''$ wide, and held together with a master link:

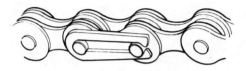

which can be taken apart without special tools; the other for derailleur equipped bikes, is $3/32''$ wide, and has no master link (it would catch in the rear gear cluster), so that a special chain riveting tool is needed to take it apart or put it together:

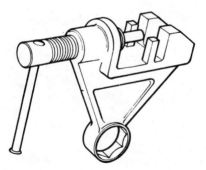

Removal and Replacement

Chains should be replaced every two years on bikes that see constant use, and every three years on bikes that see average service. Although the chain may look perfectly sound, the tiny bit of wear on each rivet and plate adds up to a considerable alteration in size. A worn chain will chip teeth on (expensive) gear sprockets. To test for wear, remove chain (see below) and lay on table with rollers parallel to surface. Hold chain with both hands about 4-5″ apart. Push hands together, and then pull apart. If you can feel slack, replace chain.

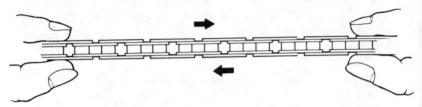

Test also for side to side deflection. It should not be more than 1″:

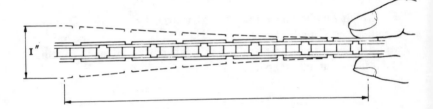

To remove and replace a master link chain find the master link

and pry it off with a screwdriver.
To remove a derailleur chain drive out a rivet with a chain tool:

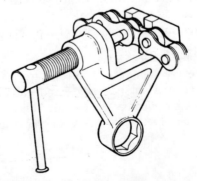

Be sure that the point of the chain tool centers exactly on the rivet. *Do not drive the rivet all the way out.* Go only as far as the outside plate. Stop frequently to check progress. Once rivet is near chain plate I like to free link by inserting a thin screwdriver and twisting gently:

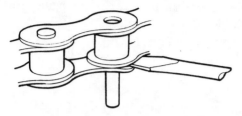

Another method is simply to twist the chain. Be careful that you do not bend the plates. To replace rivet, reverse tool:

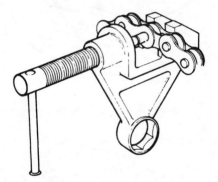

Again, be careful how far you go, or the link will jam (see Troubleshooting to fix).

Fitting

Most new chains need to be shortened in order to fit properly. On a non-derailleur bike it should be set so that there is ½" up and down play in the chain with the rear wheel in proper position:

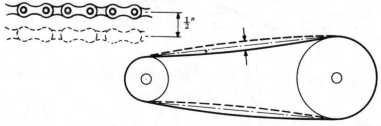

On a derailleur bike, the chain needs to be long enough to fit over the large front and back sprockets, and short enough to fit on the small front and rear sprockets. The less tension the better, but be careful the derailleur does not double up on itself. Remove links from end of chain that has two plates with no roller between them. Some adjustment can be made by changing wheel position with adjustable blocks on the rear dropouts:

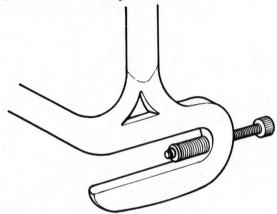

Lubrication

The scheme for lubrication depends on what kind of lubricant you use.

In my opinion the best is a petroleum distillate spray like WD-40 or LPSW-1. The greatest advantage of this stuff is that it is clean, does not attract dirt, and goes on in a flash. Apply every 1 or 2 weeks, and remove and soak chain clean in solvent every 2 or 3 months.

Oil is the common lubricant. The problem is that it attracts grit and the solution is to add more oil in the hope that it will float the grit away. Oil every link once a week, and remove and soak clean the chain in solvent once a month.

The most economical lubricant is paraffin, available in grocery stores. It is cleaner than oil. Remove and clean chain. Melt paraffin in coffee can, dip chain, and hang to dry so that drippings fall back into can. Once a month.

Trouble-shooting

◎ Jammed link. Use chain tool to free tight links by working the rivet back and forth a quarter-turn on the chain tool at a time. If your chain tool has a spreader slot (handy), use that:

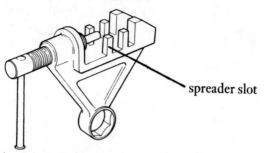

spreader slot

◎ "Klunk" sounds and/or chain jumping sprockets. Test chain for excessive wear as per above. May also be a bent sprocket tooth (see p. 191).

Rear Sprocket

All chain drive bikes have a rear sprocket. On 1- and 3-speed bikes this is a single sprocket and is extremely simple. Derailleur equipped bikes use several sprockets (also called cogs) mounted on a freewheel.

How It Works

The freewheel is in two parts, and there are two basic designs:

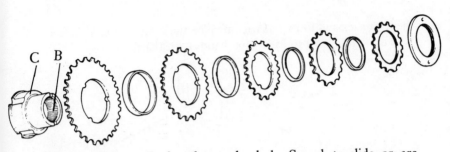

The inside part B threads on the hub. Sprockets slide or are threaded on the outside part C. The freewheel is ratcheted so that when the outside part C is driven clockwise by the chain, the inside part B (and hence the hub) is driven too. But when the bike is coasting, with the chain stationary, part C holds still while part B spins merrily along. This ratcheting is accomplished through the use of·a clever maze of ball bearings, pins, springs, and other minute and complex parts inside the freewheel.

Adjustment

Periodically check for chipped or bent teeth by looking at them in profile:

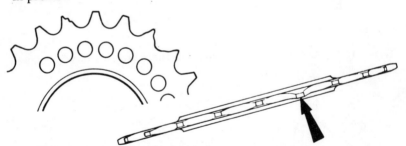

Replace cogs that have chipped or broken teeth, or an uneven U between teeth. Straighten bent teeth by removing cog (see below), gripping the bent tooth with an adjustable end wrench, and straightening:

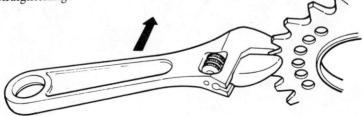

Alignment between front and back sprockets is important. Standing at the front of the bike and sighting between the two front sprockets, you should see the center cog of the back gear cluster:

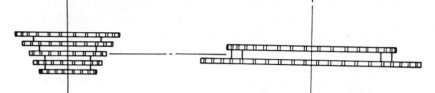

If back sprocket is too far out, so you can see the 2nd or 1st largest rear cog, the front sprocket must be moved out. This can only be done by installing a longer bottom bracket axle (p. 190). If you have Ashtabula one-piece cranks (p. 186) there is nothing you can do at all.

If back sprocket is too far in, so you can see the 4th ot 5th largest rear cog, it must be moved out. This is done by removing the freewheel (p. 199), installing a shim (bike stores), the freewheel again, and then possibly another shim so that the freewheel will clear the drop-outs. All this stuff usually makes it hard to get the wheel back in and may necessitate a little judicious bending. It is better to let a bike shop deal with problems of this sort.

Lubrication

A bi-weekly shot of a petroleum distillate spray like WD-40 or LPSW-1 is best. Remove freewheel (see below) and soak clean in solvent once a year.

Oil: a few drops once a month. Remove and soak clean in solvent every six months.

Removal and Disassembly

This requires a freewheel remover. There are two types, pronged and splined:

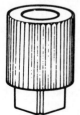

Look at your freewheel to see which kind you need. Remove wheel (p. 157). Remove nut and washers from freewheel side of axle. Quick release hubs: remove conical nut and spring from shaft of skewer and place spring in a jar. Fit freewheel remover. If it won't go on you may have a spacer nut. Remove with a wrench while holding axle stationary with another wrench on the left side cone or locknut. Fit freewheel remover into slots or splines. Replace nut on axle or skewer and screw down hand-tight. Use a wrench on the freewheel remover to break the freewheel loose (counter-clockwise). This may be difficult. As soon as it comes loose, remove freewheel and spin it off by hand.

Replacing freewheel. *Note:* a new freewheel or sprockets requires a matching new chain, especially if the existing chain is more than a year old. A stretched chain will probably kick up on new sprockets. Also, if you are getting a new freewheel, read the chapter on gears. You may be interested in changing gear ratios. If you do this, be sure to check chain tension after installing freewheel (p 195). To replace a freewheel simply screw it on, being extremely careful not to strip the threads on the hub. Snug down with the freewheel remover secured by the axle bolt but do not bear down hard; it will tighten as you ride.

Changing cogs: For this you need a sprocket remover (bike shops) and, if you are removing all the sprockets, a freewheel vise (ditto). Incidentally, if you want a number of different gear ratios it is much simpler to have two fully set up freewheels with different gear ratios than to keep diddling with individual sprockets. However, if you are experimenting to work out the combination of cogs which is best for you and are impatient with bike shops (they can do this job very quickly), then by all means proceed. Removing a cog is simple – it unscrews or slides off the freewheel – but tools for the job vary considerably in design. Follow the instructions given with your particular tool. If you change the small or large cog, be sure to check chain tension (p. 195) after reassembly.

Dismantle freewheel. Uh-uh. This is another of those profitless jobs. If the freewheel goes, replace it.

Trouble-shooting

⊙ A "klunk" two or three times per complete revolution of the front sprocket. May be a bent tooth on a freewheel sprocket. Check as per above.

◎ Freewheel won't freewheel. Try soaking in solvent to free up innards. No? Replace it.

◎ Freewheel turns but hub doesn't. Spin cranks while holding bike stationary and look carefully at freewheel. If both parts spin around the hub, threads on hub are stripped. New hub. If outside part of freewheel spins around inside part, freewheel is clogged up (frozen) or broken. Try soaking in solvent. No? Replace.

Gear Changer Systems

Except for the two-speed pedal-operated rear hubs, gear changer systems typically include a shift trigger, lever, or twistgrip, a cable, and the gear changing mechanism, of which there are two kinds, internal rear hub, and derailleur.

Multi-speed internally Geared Rear Hubs

These come in 2-, 3-, and 5-speed versions, with planetary or sun gears inside the hub. I consider these units too complicated to be worth disassembling, and so does any bike shop I have asked about doing such work. Here, for example, is an exploded view of a Sturmy Archer 3-speed hub and coaster brake combination:

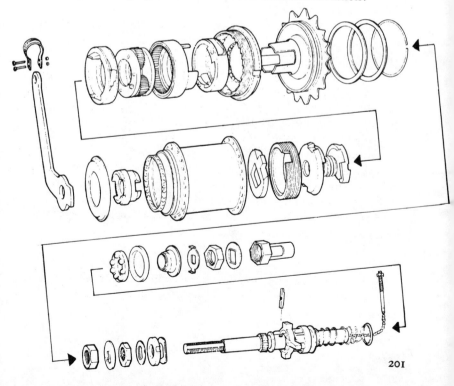

Believe me, if you run into trouble with your hub and can't solve it with routine adjustment or trouble-shooting (below), the best thing to do is remove the wheel (p. 157) and take it to a bike shop. The chance of problems arising is quite small. A regularly lubricated hub should last the life of your bike.

No adjustments are possible with 2-speed pedal-controlled hubs. There are two major brands of 3-speed hubs, Sturmy Archer, and Shimano. Service techniques for both are virtually identical, and so we will concentrate on one, the Sturmy-Archer.

How They Work

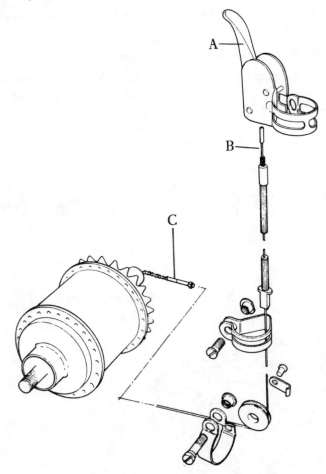

Shift trigger A connects to cable B, which in turn connects to toggle chain C on hub. Position of trigger determines gear.

Adjustment

Three-speed hubs –

To adjust a hub first run the shift lever to 3rd or H. Then take up slack in cable by loosening locknut A and screwing down barrel sleeve adjustor B:

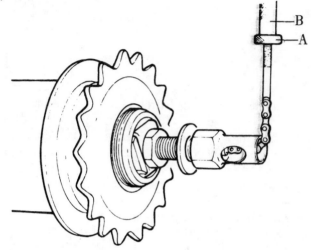

Leave cable very slightly slack. If barrel sleeve cannot do job, move the fulcrum clip which holds the cable housing on the bike frame forward:

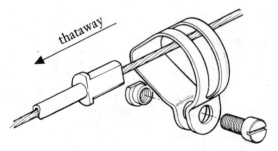

Test gears. No? Check position of indicator rod by looking through the hole in the side of the right hub nut. With the shift lever in 2nd or N position it should be exactly even with the end of the axle:

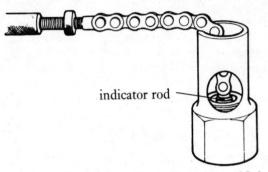

indicator rod

Adjust if necessary with barrel sleeve. Test gears. No? Remove barrel sleeve altogether. Check that indicator rod is screwed finger-tight fully into hub. Reassemble and adjust as above. No? Turn to Trouble-shooting, this section (p. 208).

Five-speed hubs –

For the righthand shift lever, follow the same procedure as for the 3-speed hub, above.

For lefthand shift lever, set it all the way forward and screw cable connector to bellcrank B two or three turns:

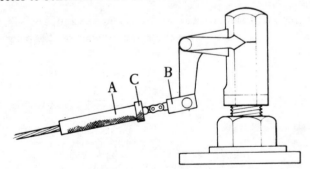

Then run shift lever all the way back, and take slack out of cable with cable connector. Secure with locknut C.

Lubrication

A tablespoon of oil inside hub once a month. I strongly recommend a quality oil such as is sold in bike and gun shops. Some household and other cheap oils leave behind a sticky residue when the oil evaporates. This is the last thing in the world you want. Once a month use a little petroleum distillate spray or a few drops of oil on the trigger control, cable, and inside the cable housing.

Disassembly and Replacement

Hub –
   Remove wheel   (p. 157) and take it to a bike shop.
Cable –
   Needs replacement when it becomes frayed, the housing kinked or broken, or exhibits suspicious political tendencies.

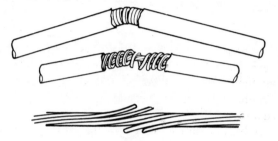

Run shift selector to 3rd or H. Disconnect barrel sleeve from indicator and loosen fulcrum clip (for illustration, see Adjustment above). To free cable from a

   Trigger: shift to 1st or L, pry up holding plate A with a small screwdriver, and push cable *in* until nipple clears ratchet plate:

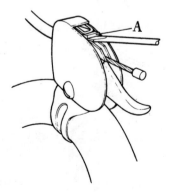

and then pull cable out. Remove entire cable and housing assembly from bike and set aside fulcrum sleeve.

Twist-grip: first take off the spring S with a screwdriver:

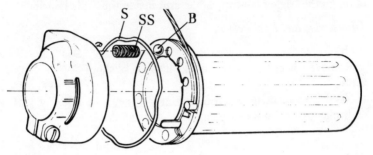

Slide the twist-grip off the handlebar and catch the ball bearing B and spring SS if they fall out. Release nipple from slot, and remove cable and cable housing assembly from bike.

Top tube lever: undo the cable anchor bolt near the hub:

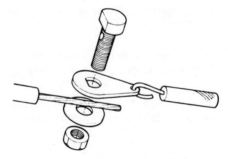

Unscrew the two shift lever halves A and B, and lift casing C away from bike:

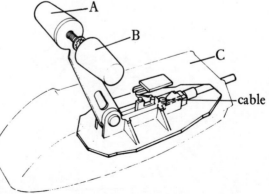

Push cable in to free nipple from slot and thread out cable.

Note: Take the old cable with you to the shop when getting replacement. This kind of cable comes in a variety of lengths. To replace a cable to a

Trigger: place the fulcrum sleeve on cable housing and thread through fulcrum clip. Pry up trigger control plate, insert cable through hole in trigger casing, and slip nipple into slot on ratchet. Run cable over pulley wheel if you have one, and attach to toggle chain. Shift to 3rd or H. Position fulcrum clip so cable is just slightly slack and tighten. Adjust if necessary as per above.

Twist-grip: insert nipple into slot. Grease and replace spring and ball bearing. Slide twist-grip on handlebar and secure with spring clip. Use a small screwdriver to work the spring clip in. Run cable over pulley wheel if you have one, and attach to toggle chain. Shift selector to 3rd or H and adjust as per above.

To top tube lever: thread cable through slot until nipple catches. Replace cable housing or run cable over pulley wheel, depending on the kind of system you have. Connect cable to anchor bolt, shift to 3rd or H, and adjust as per above. Replace casing, and screw together handle halves.

If you have a bashed or recalcitrant shift control the best thing is to replace it. They are not expensive. To replace.

Trigger: disconnect cable (see above) and undo bolt B:

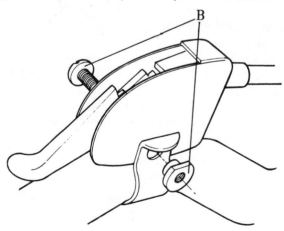

Twist-grip or top tube lever: I recommend replacing with a standard handlebar trigger, which is a much better mechanical design and more reliable. To remove old unit disconnect cable (see above) and undo bolt B:

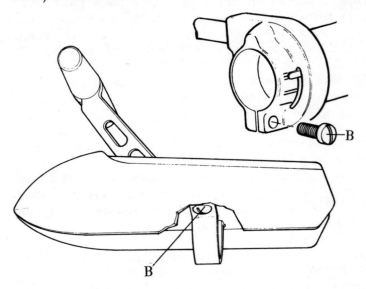

Trouble-shooting

No gear at all (pedals spin freely) or slips in and out of gear.
⊙ Is gear in proper adjustment (p. 203)?
⊙ Is cable binding? Check by disconnecting barrel sleeve at hub (p. 204) and working cable back and forth through housing. Replace (p. 205) if it binds.
⊙ Is shift mechanism together and functioning? Stick and twist-grip models are especially prone to slippage after the track for the ball bearing becomes worn:

◎ Insides of hubs may have gotten gunked up through the use of too heavy or household oils so that pawls are stuck. Try putting in kerosene or penetrating oil and jiggling everything around. No? ◎Uncle. Remove wheel (p. 157) and take to a bike shop.

Derailleurs –

A derailleur system includes a shift lever, usually mounted on the down tube, but also on the top tube, or the stem, or at the handlebar ends,

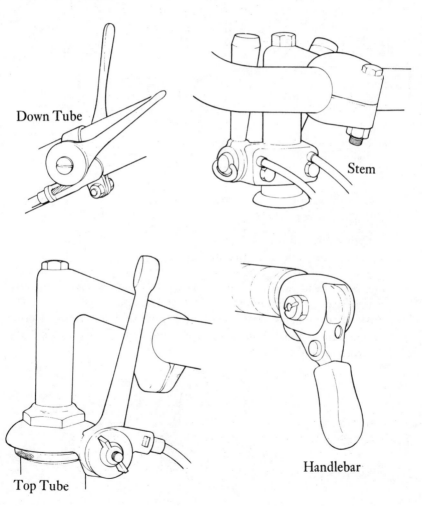

Down Tube

Stem

Top Tube

Handlebar

a thin cable and (sometimes) cable housing, and a front or rear gear changer (derailleur) through which the chain passes. When the shift lever is actuated, the derailleur moves sideways and forces the chain onto a different sprocket.

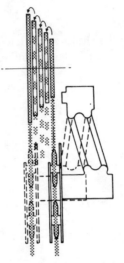

Although we are dealing here with a system, it will simplify everything to take it piece by piece first, and then deal with it as a whole.

Shift Lever

How It Works – Adjustment – Removal and Replacement

The shift lever should be set so that you can move it without undue strain, but be stiff enough to hold fast against spring pressure from the derailleur. This adjustment is made with the tension screw A:

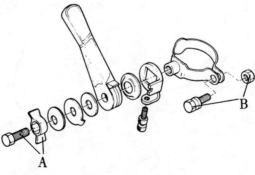

Some tension screws have a slot for a screwdriver (or coin), others have wings, and others have wire loops. All function the same way. To dismantle the lever, simply remove the tension screw. Be sure to keep all parts in order. To remove a down tube mounted lever unit undo bolt B above.

To get a top tube lever unit off remove the stem (p. 145). A stem mounted unit comes off by undoing bolts A & B:

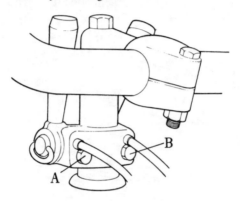

A handlebar end unit requires first removing trim nut A:

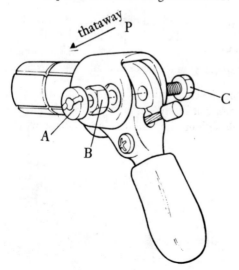

and then nut B and screw C. Then loosen Allen screw (6 mm) located at point P inside selector body, and remove unit.

Cables –

Adjustment

Cables of derailleur systems are frequently exposed, thin, and take a hell of a beating. Check them often for fraying:

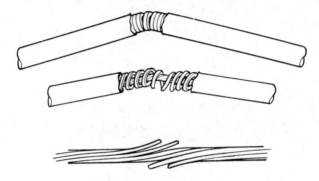

Adjustment is needed when the shift lever has to be pulled all the way back to engage the large sprocket. Place the shift lever forward so that the chain is on the smallest sprocket. Some systems have a barrel adjustor, either at the derailleur or at the shift lever:

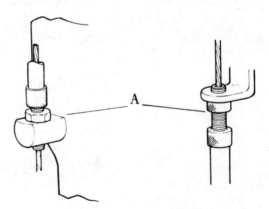

Undo the locknut A and move the barrel adjustor up until slack is removed from cable. If this will not do the job, turn barrel adjustor back down fully home, and reset cable anchor bolt.

All derailleurs, front and back, use a cable anchor bolt or screw to hold the cable. Here is the location (CB) on four representative types:

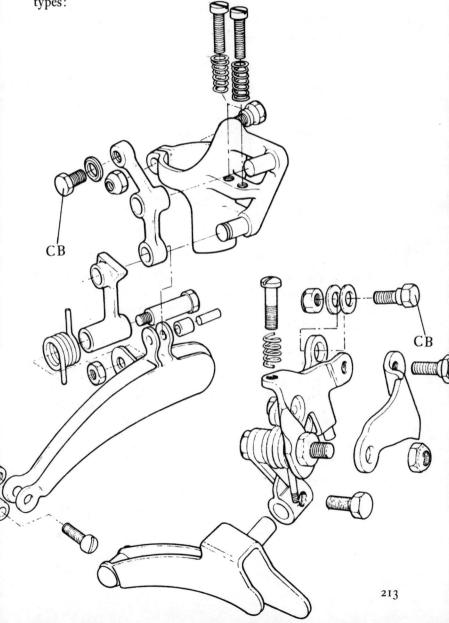

CB

CB

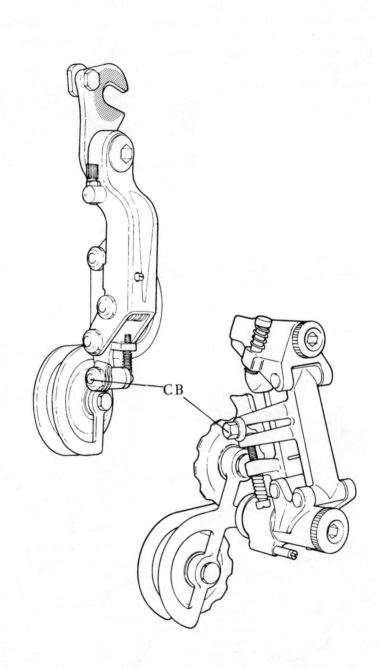

CB

Loosen the bolt, take the slack out of the cable, pulling it through with pliers if necessary, and retighten bolt.

Removal and Replacement

Run chain to smallest sprocket. Screw home barrel adjustor, if you have one. Undo cable anchor bolt and thread cable out of derailleur. Check cable housings (not on all models) for kinks and breaks. Remove cable from lever by threading it out:

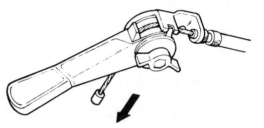

Reassembly: *Note:* do not cut new cable to size until it is installed or it will jam when going into cable housings. If you are cutting new cable housing, be sure to get the jaws of the cutter *between* the wire coils of the housing:

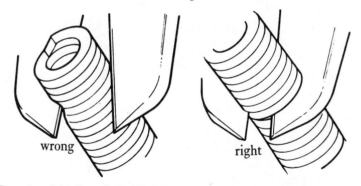

wrong   right

Start by threading through shift lever, and then through down tube tunnel, cable stops, cable housings, and whatever else is in your particular system. As you pass the cable through cable housings, be sure to twist it so that the strands do not unravel:

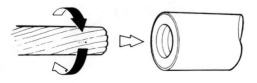

Finish at derailleur. Move shift lever to forward position, make sure that cable housing ferrules (if you have them) are seated properly, and attach cable to cable anchor bolt.

Trouble-shooting

Cable problems are evinced by delayed shifts, or no shifts at all. In any case, the procedure is the same: undo the cable anchor bolt and slide the cable around by hand, looking for sticky spots. Check carefully for fraying, and for kinks in the cable housing.

Derailleurs - Front

How They Work

There is a metal cage through which the chain passes as it feeds onto the front sprocket. The cage can be moved from side to side, and by pressing on the side of the chain, shifts it from sprocket to sprocket:

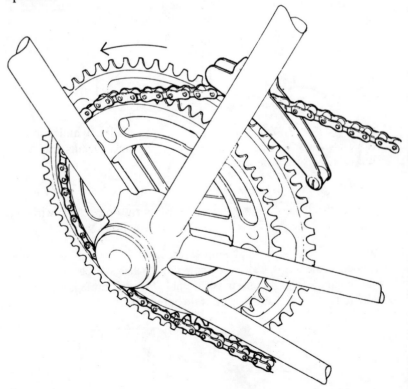

Virtually all derailleurs are built as a parallelogram. Heh. This design is used to keep the sides of the cage A straight up and down as the cage is moved from side to side on the pivot bolt P:

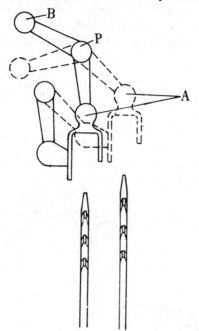

The cage is moved by pulling with a cable at point B, and when the cable is released, spring tension pushes it back. Details may vary, but this is the basic design.

Adjustment

The changer as a whole must be properly positioned, with the outer side of the cage about $\frac{1}{4}''$ to $\frac{1}{2}''$ above the sprocket:

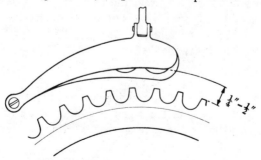

Raise or lower the unit by undoing the mounting bolt (S). The sides of the cage should follow the curvature of the sprocket. Some cages are adjustable in this respect, others (perfectly good ones) are not. Those that are usually swivel on a post between the cage and changer. Sometimes the post comes off the changer, and sometimes off the cage. Either way, there will be a locking bolt like C:

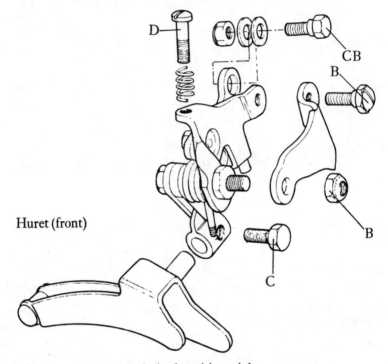

Huret (front)

Loosen, rotate cage to desired position, tighten.

Side to side travel of the cage must be set. First check that cable is properly adjusted (p. 212). Front derailleurs fall into two design categories, those with 2 adjusting screws, and those with 1.
Look at yours to determine the type.

One-screw derailleurs

Run chain to largest back and smallest front sprockets. The first adjustment is made with the cage positioning bolt C (above).
Loosen it, and move the cage so that the left side just clears the

chain. Tighten. Now back off the adjusting screw D 3 or 4 turns. Run the chain to the smallest back and largest front sprockets. Using the shift lever, position the cage so that the right side just clears the chain. Turn down adjusting screw D until resistance is felt, and stop.

Two-screw derailleurs

If you can't find your adjusting screws easily, get down close to the unit and watch it carefullly as you wiggle the shift lever back and forth. Each time the body of the changer reaches the end of its travel it will be resting on a spring-loaded screw or knurled ring:

On Campagnolo units they are the screws E & D:

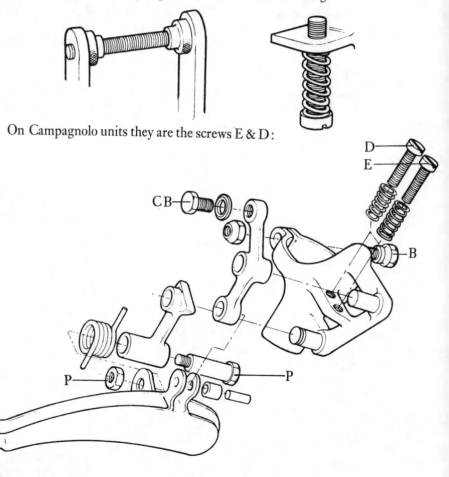

Run chain to largest and smallest front sprockets. It should just clear the left side of the cage. Adjust left side (low gear) adjusting screw (D, above) as necessary until it does. Now run chain to smallest back and largest front sprockets. It should just clear the right side of the cage. Adjust right side (high gear) adjusting screw (E, below) as necessary until it does. Test operation of gears. Sometimes it is necessary to set the high gear adjustment a little wide to get the chain to climb up on the big sprocket – but be cautious, or the chain will throw off the sprocket.

Lubrication

A little petroleum distillate spray or a few drops of oil on the pivot bolts once a month. If the unit becomes particularly dirty, take it off (see below) and soak it clean in kerosene or other solvent.

Replace

Remove chain (p.193). Undo cable anchor bolt and slip off cable (p. 215). Now undo mounting bolt(s) B and remove unit:

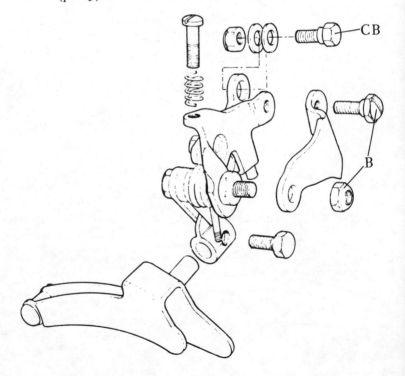

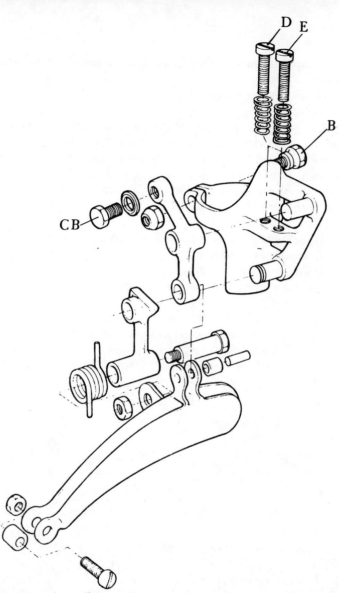

Reverse to replace. Other units may have different mounting bolts but their function will be clear.

Trouble-shooting

Most of the difficulties experienced with the front changer are actually caused by problems elsewhere in the power train. I am assuming that you have already set your changer as per Adjustment, above.

Chain rubs side of cage.

◎ Is shift lever tight (p. 210)?

◎ Can you stop rubbing by diddling with shift lever? For example, the amount of right travel necessary to shift the chain from the left (small) sprocket to the right sprocket may leave the cage too far to the right when the chain is on the large back sprocket, and cause the chain to rub the left side of the cage. In fact, it is frequently necessary with front changers to move the cage back just a trifle after a shift has been completed (p. 210).

◎ Is the sprocket warped (p. 186)? Or loose (p. 189)?

Chain throws off sprocket.

◎ Is shift lever tight (p. 210)?

◎ Cage travel may be set too far out. Adjust it slightly (p. 217).

◎ Is chain old? Test (p. 193).

◎ Are sprocket teeth bent (p. 191)?

◎ Are front and rear sprockets in alignment (p. 199)?

◎ If chain continually over-rides big front sprocket, take an adjustable end wrench and bend the leading tip of the outside cage in very slightly – about $\frac{1}{16}$″:

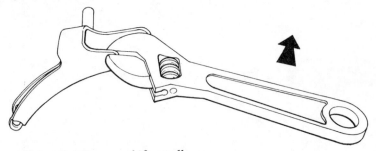

Delayed shifts or no shifts at all.

◎ Are pivot bolts clean? Try a little spray or oil.

◎ Is spring intact and in place?

◎ Is cable sticking or broken (p. 212)?

◎ If pivot bolts are adjustable, as P is on this Campagnolo unit (**opposite**) undo locknut, back P off one-eighth turn, reset locknut.

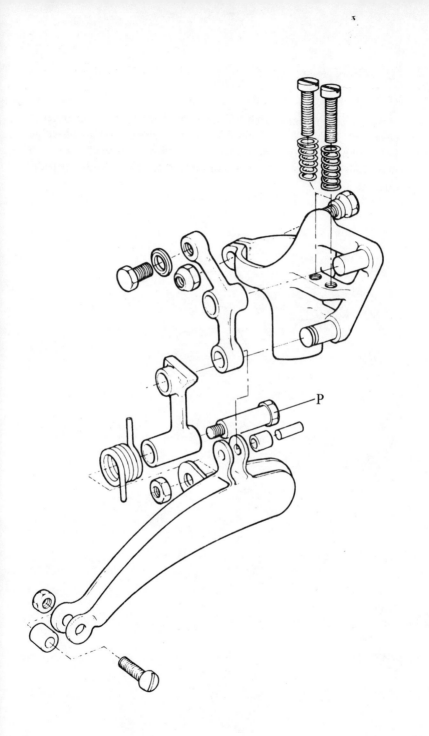

P

How They Work

As the chain comes back off the bottom of the front sprocket it passes through the rear derailleur on two chain rollers. The cage holding the rollers is fastened to the main body of the changer by a pivot bolt P, and is under constant spring tension so as to keep the chain taut:

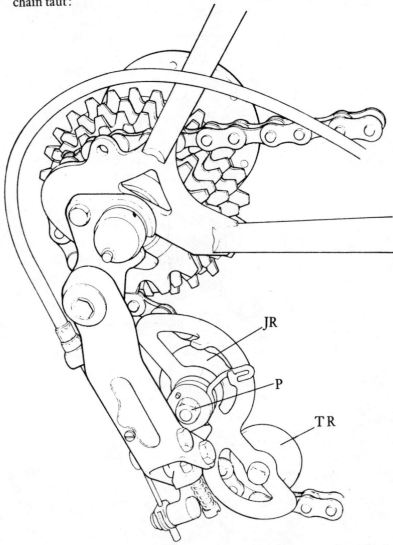

The lower roller is the tension roller (TR), the upper the jockey roller (JR). The position of the cage, and hence of the chain on the rear gear cluster, is determined by the changer body:

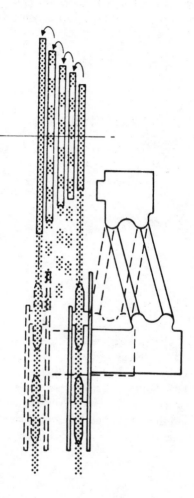

The changer body is under constant spring tension to carry it to the smallest sprocket. It is restrained from doing so by a cable and shift lever.

Derailleurs come in two basic designs, box, like the Huret Allvit or Simplex, and bare parallelogram, like the Campagnolo:

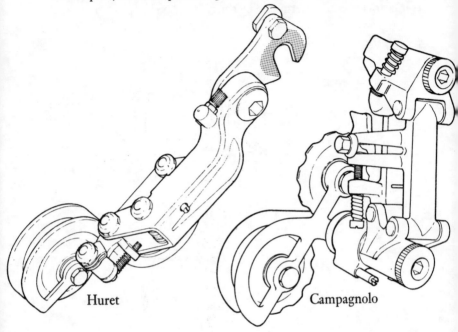

Huret   Campagnolo

Adjustment

Position of changer with respect to bike –

The body of the changer should form an angle with the vertical of about 20° to 30°. Many derailleurs are not adjustable in this respect and are held by spring tension against a stop (Campagnolo, Simplex). Others like the Huret Allvit can be adjusted by loosening locknut A and then pivot bolt P (see opposite page).

Chain rollers should align with the chain:

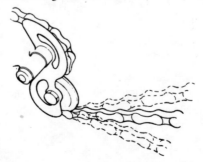

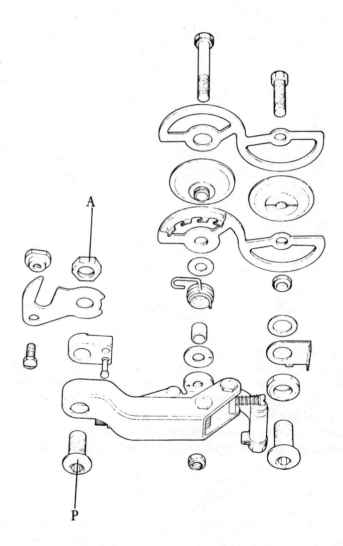

If your derailleur is fastened to a mounting plate, remove it (see below), clamp in a vise, and bend it with an adjustable end wrench:

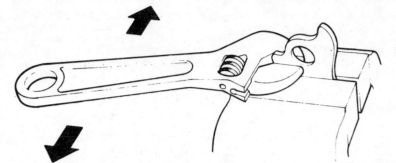

If your derailleur is bolted straight into the frame drop-out, snug wrench around the chain rollers and bend into alignment:

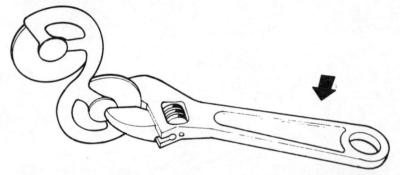

Bear in mind that this is a fairly drastic measure. I am assuming that the derailleur was bent in an accident, and that you have no choice. The alternative is replacement (see below), which you should consider if the old derailleur is on the way out. Box changers such as the Huret or Simplex are inexpensive and quite reliable, and a working derailleur, no matter how plastic and cheap, is miles ahead of a fancy job which is one shift away from disintegration.

Note: if it is a brand new derailleur which is out of alignment then the fault is with the frame drop-out. You can bend this into line yourself with an adjustable end wrench the same as you would bend the derailleur mount (above), but this is a very serious matter which should be left to a bike shop. Bending does cause metal fatigue, and if the rear drop-out were to shear unexpectedly you might have an accident.

— Side to side travel of derailleur.

First check with chain on smallest rear and biggest front sprockets, and with rear derailleur shift lever all the way forward, that there is only a little slack in the cable. Take up or give slack through barrel adjustor and/or cable anchor bolt (p. 212).

The derailleur needs to be set so that side to side travel is stopped short of throwing the chain into the wheel or off the small sprocket. This is done with two adjusting screws or knurled rings, and here is their location on 3 typical units (high gear – E, low gear – D):

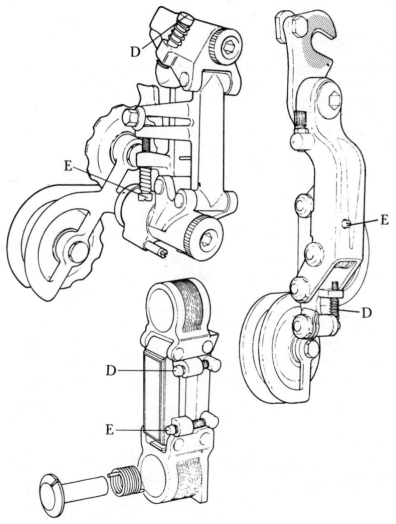

If your derailleur isn't included here, get down close to it and run it back and forth, seeing which adjusting screw does what. OK, now: if derailleur goes too far, throwing chain off, set in position with shift lever so that jockey wheel lines up with sprocket on the side you are working on, and turn in appropriate adjusting screw or knurled ring until resistance is felt. Stop. If derailleur does not go far enough, back the appropriate adjusting screw off until it does. If this does not work, check to make absolutely sure adjusting screw is backed off. Yes? Turn to Trouble-shooting, p. 221, for what to do next.

— Spring tension for roller cage.

Spring tension on the roller cage should be sufficient to keep the chain taut when in high gear. No tighter. Excess tension will cause unnecessary drag and rapid wear. On the other hand, too loose a chain will skip. If you have this problem and the chain tension seems OK, check the chain itself for wear (p. 193). Worn chains skip.

Adjustment procedure varies according to type of derailleur. Many have the spring set on a hook on the roller cage:

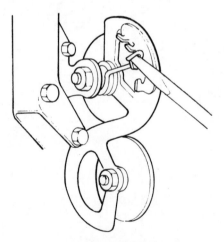

Move it carefully with pliers or screwdriver.

On the Simplex, remove screw and dust cap (not on all models) from bottom pivot bolt A (see opposite page).

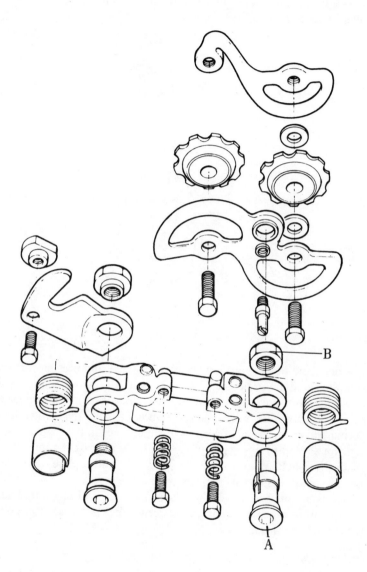

Loosen locknut B, use a metric Allen wrench to turn A clockwise for more tension, counter-clockwise for less, reset locknut.

On a Campagnolo unit, first remove wheel. Then remove tension roller by undoing bolt G:

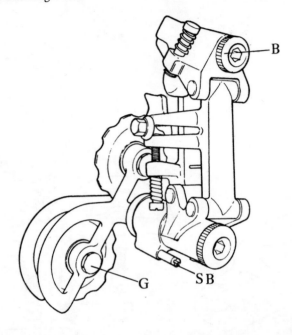

Use one hand to hang onto the chain roller cage and prevent it from spinning, and unscrew the cage stop bolt SB. Now let the cage unwind (about one-half to three-quarters of a turn). Remove cage pivot bolt with Allen wrench and lift off cage. Note that protruding spring end engages one of a series of small holes in the cage. Rotate cage forward until spring fits into next hole (see opposite page) Replace pivot bolt. Wind cage back $\frac{1}{2}$ - $\frac{3}{4}$ turn and replace cage stop bolt. Replace tension roller and go back to the races.

Shimano units: Remove wheel, tension roller, and cage stop bolt. Rotate entire cage one turn against spring. Replace cage stop bolt, tension roller, wheel.

Lubrication

Petroleum spray: once a month on the jockey and tension rollers, pivot bolts, and cables. Once a year remove and soak clean in solvent.

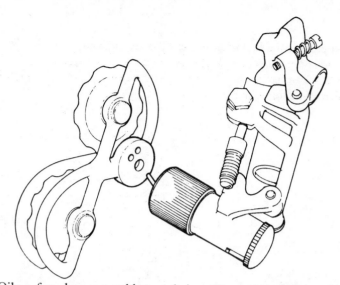

Oil: a few drops monthly on chain rollers, pivot bolts, cables. Soak clean in solvent every six months. Regrease wheel bearings, if you have them (p. 234).

Removal and Disassembly

Disconnect cable from anchor bolt (pp. 213).

Remove tension roller by undoing bolt G (opposite page and below). Undo mounting bolt B (Campagnolo) or slacken axle nut and remove adapter screw AS (Huret Allvit) according to how your unit is mounted (opposite and next pages).

Disassembly: the parts that need this regularly are the chain rollers. Otherwise do it only to replace parts. Chain rollers: get jockey roller off (tension roller is already off).

On the Campagnolo this is done by undoing the jockey roller bolt just like the bolt for the tension roller. On the Huret it is necessary to first unsnap the cage spring:

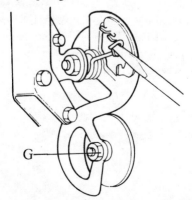

and then unscrew the cage mounting bolt CB:

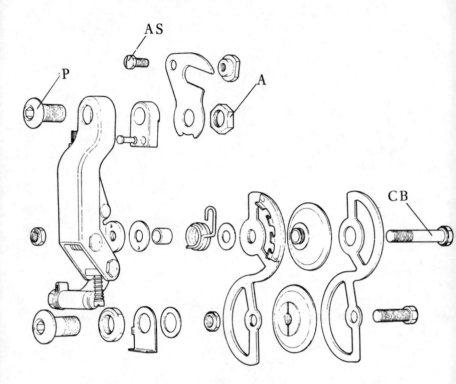

Be careful! of those shims and whatnots. Keep track of their order.
There are two kinds of chain rollers, those with washers and a
metal sleeve, and those with a hub and ball bearings:

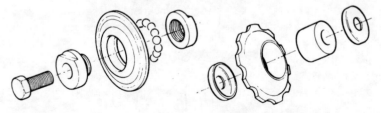

If you have the ball bearing type, disassemble the hub and remove the bearings. Both types: clean in solvent. Ball bearing type reassembly: lay one cone flat on table, place chain roller over it. Apply petroleum spray or grease. Put in ball bearings. More lubricant. Screw on second cone.

For the rest of it, the degree of disassembly possible, as well as the technique, varies somewhat from model to model. We'll do three: the Huret, Campagnolo, and Simplex.

The Huret Allvit:

Undo locknut A and remove pivot bolt P with Allen wrench. Keep parts in order. Next: undo the upper lever arm bolt D:

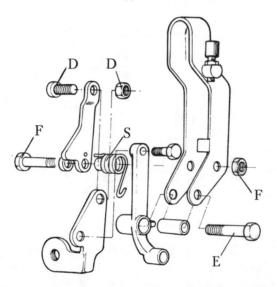

and then lower lever arm bolt E. Remove lever arm, and use pliers to pry spring S off changer body. Then remove bolt F to remove spring S. Replace any parts to be replaced. Clean everything in solvent.

Reassembly: *Note:* Be sure to set all locknuts with sufficient play for smooth derailleur operation. Assemble movement arm spring S, bushing, spacer, at housing and insert bolt F, secure with locknut. Replace spring hook on changer body. Put lever arm in place and secure with bolts D and E.

Reassemble cage (see above for illustrations): mounting bolt CB,

outside cage, jockey roller, inside cage (has hooks for cage spring–
these face changer body), washer, cage spring and bushing, washer;
screw this assembly into the cage mounting plate. Set cage spring
with screwdriver. replace pivot bolt, stop plate, mounting plate.
Mount derailleur on frame. Replace tension toller.Re-engage cable
Adjust side to side play as necessary (p. 229).

The Campagnolo

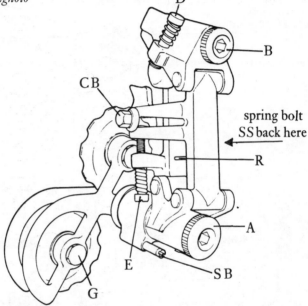

Hang onto chain roller cage to prevent it from spinning and
remove cage stop bolt SB. Let cage unwind (about one-half to three-
quarters of a turn). Remove cage pivot bolt with Allen wrench and
lift off cage. Slide out pivot bolt A and spring. Back off high gear
adjusting screw E to minimize changer body spring tension, and
undo spring bolt SS. Replace parts, clean everything in solvent.
Reassembly: screw in spring bolt SS while holding changer body
spring R in position. Replace cage spring and slide in pivot bolt.
Put cage on changer with two half moon sides next to changer.Put
nut on pivot bolt. Rotate cage back one-half to three-quarters of a
turn and screw in cage stop bolt SB. Replace jockey roller. Mount
derailleur on frame. Replace tension roller, cable. Adjust side to
side travel as above (p. 229).

236

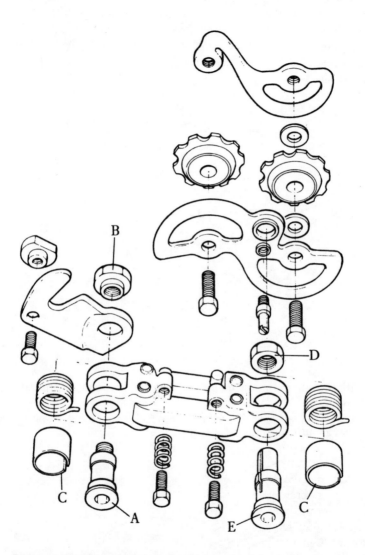

Remove dust caps from pivot bolts A and E. Spring off clips C (not all models). Undo locknut B for main arm pivot bolt A and remove bolt and spring. Ditto for locknut D and cage pivot bolt E. Some Simplex models have a circlip which can be removed so the anchor bolt F will slide out:

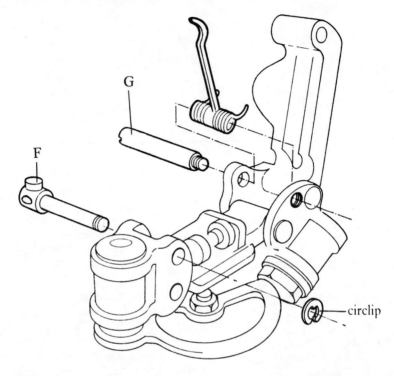

With the outer arm hinged up to relieve tension, unscrew the spring pivot pin G.

Other models lack this feature, in which case prise the spring up with a screwdriver:

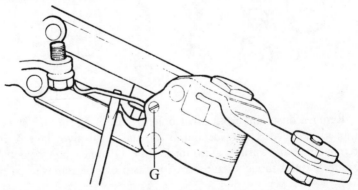

and then unscrew spring pivot pin G. Clean everything in solvent and replace defective parts.

To reassemble: Put main body spring in place and screw in spring pivot pin. Push down outer arm and secure with anchor bolt and circlip, or set spring in place with screwdriver. Put in cage pivot bolt and spring. Put on locknut and cage, and give cage pivot bolt one-half turn to right for proper spring tension before setting locknut. Repeat process for main arm pivot bolt, spring, and locknut. Fasten jockey roller to cage. Mount derailleur on frame. Mount tension roller, and then connect shift cable. Adjust side to side travel of derailleur as necessary (p. 229).

Trouble-shooting

Derailleur is sticky, won't always shift, sometimes shifts unexpectedly.

◎ Is shift lever working smoothly but with enough friction to hold derailleur in place (p.211)?

◎ Are cables sticking (p. 212)?

◎ Are pivot bolts lubricated and clean? On some models (Campagnolo, Huret, among others) these bolts can be adjusted:

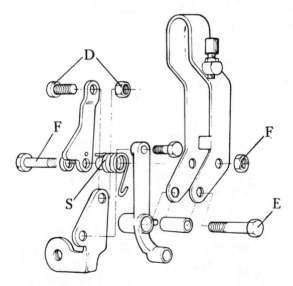

Undo locknuts for bolts D, E, and F, undo bolts one-eighth turn, reset locknuts.

Derailleur will not go far enough.

◎ Is cable slightly slack with shift lever all the way forward (p. 229)?

◎ Are adjusting screws properly set (p. 229)?

◎ Does cable slide easily (p. 216)?

◎ Is pivot or main changer spring broken?

⌒ Are chain rollers lined up with chain (p. 226)?

◎ Try to wiggle the derailleur unit by hand. Can you push it to the desired position?

Yes:

works are gummed up. Clean in solvent and lubricate with spray or oil. Adjust (not possible with all models) by undoing pivot bolts one-eighth turn and resetting. (Illustration above).

No:

if it won't reach the big rear cog, remove mounting plate and bend it in a vise.

if it won't reach the little rear cog, bend mounting plate, or put in shims at the mounting bolt.

Chain throws off cogs.

◎ Are adjusting screws set properly (p. 229)?

◎ Are any teeth worn or bent (p.191, 198)?

◎ Is chain good (p. 193)?

◎ If chain is skipping, is spring tension for roller cage sufficient (p. 230)?

◎ Is roller cage aligned with chain (p. 226)?

P is the chain pulley, one being placed at either end of the crank-shaft, and capable of freely revolving thereon, except when jambed by the shallow rollers, R. These rollers lie in a cavity formed by a circular recess in the pulley and a steel disc, D, which is shaped off on four sides so as to form alternately hollows and wedges. The disc, D, is a fixture on the crank-shaft. When the latter moves forward in the direction shown by the arrows, the rollers, R, are jambed between the disc and the inner surface of the pulley, P, and the whole of the parts, pulley included, run solid. The machine is then driven. On the contrary, when D is turned in the opposite direction, the rollers pass into the hollow spaces, and there simply rotate without jambing. This also happens when the crank-shaft, with the disc D, is held stationary as in running down hill, in which case the pulley P runs on, rotating the rollers in the hollows as already explained.

Power Train – Trouble-shooting Index

Noises

First make sure that noise is coming from power train by coasting bike. If noise continues it is probably a brake (p. 106) or hub (p. 174) problem. If noise persists, try to determine if it comes from the front (crankset), the chain, or the rear sprocket(s). Do this by disconnecting the chain (p 194) and spinning the various parts.

Grinding noises:

Front –
◉ Bottom bracket bearings OK (pp. 186, 189)?
◉ Pedal bearings OK (p. 181)?
◉ Chain rubbing derailleur?
◉ Front sprocket rubbing cage or chainstays (p. 222)?
Back –
◉ Wheel bearings OK (p. 176)?
◉ Freewheel OK (p. 197)?

Clicks or Clunks:

One for every revolution of crankset –
◉ Pedal tight (p. 181)?
◉ Crank(s) tight (p. 183)?
◉ Bottom bracket bearings OK (pp. 186,189)?
◉ Are teeth on sprocket(s) bent (pp 191,198)?
Two or three for every revolution of the crankset –
◉ Are teeth on rear sprocket(s) bent (p. 198)?
◉ Is chain worn or frozen (p. 193)?
No go. Pedals and chain spin uselessly –
  Three-speeds, see p. 208.
  Ten-speeds, see p. 201.
Delayed shifts, no shifts, or not all gears
  Three-speeds, see p. 208.
  Ten-speeds, see p. 239.

For all other problems consult the trouble-shooting section for the part which is malfunctioning.

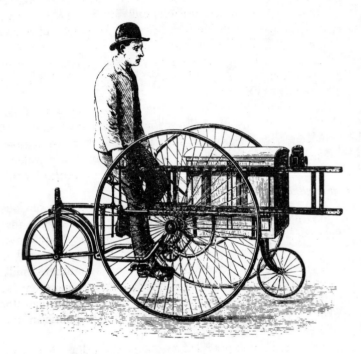

Tricycle carriers like this late 1800 s model
are what we need now.

6. Dream * Ramode * Sunfighter * Dream * Birthright *

Everybody has dreams and here is one of mine: cars are banned from central areas of all major metropolitan regions. Each city provides free bicycles (with adjustable seats and handlebars) scattered about to be used as needed. Because cities can buy enough bikes at a time to make special orders feasible, each city has a bike with a unique and readily identifiable frame design. All bolts and screws have left-hand threads, like the light bulbs in subway stations, to discourage the stealing of parts for private use. There are repair centers throughout town, as well as special racks in which bikes in need of servicing can be left.

Schemes something like this are already working with a fair degree of success in Europe. Amsterdam is a blizzard of public and private bicycles. The chances for such a sequence here are remote. There is just too much money to be made from cars and petroleum products. That you and I pay a stiff price in life and health for this profit making is immaterial.

In the struggle of bike versus car the bike emerges an obvious winner in economic and ecological terms. Logic would suggest that the bicycle be favored as a mode of transport, but as anybody knows this is not so. This is the age of the motor car. It is also a period in which ecological causes have become as sound as mother's milk. Hardly a Sunday goes by without some politician hopping on the ecological bandwagon and puffing his way on a bike through the opening of a special 'Bikeway.' But rare indeed is the politician who rides to work.

A classic example was provided by John V. Lindsay, Mayor of New York, who led a parade of bicyclists for 14 blocks before returning to his limousine. The occasion was the creation of 'Bikeways' on some major avenues. What this means is that there are little signs posted along the avenues which say 'Bikeway'. Practically speaking, these make absolutely no difference whatsoever, as any bike rider who has to mix it up with NYC traffic can testify.

All is not gloom however, and the 'Bikeways' boom has a lot to recommend it. Bikeways come in different classes:

Class I   – A separate lane for bikes only.
Class II   – A restricted lane in a street with no autos allowed.
Class III – Streets with slotted speed bumps to slow down but not

eliminate autos.

Class IV – Painted lane on a pedestrian path.

Class V – Signs on regular thoroughfares which say 'Bikeway'.

Class I and II bikeways are the only meaningful types, and where implemented have been a great success. The city of Davis, California, for example, has had Class I bikeways on the University of California campus, and Class II bikeways throughout town, since 1966. Davis has a population of 24,000 and approximately 18,000 bicycles. One survey found that during rush hour 40% of the traffic was bicycles, and 90% of the riders were adults.

There are approximately 15,000 miles of bike paths in the U.S. of A., with 200,000 "planned" for 1975. These come in all shapes and sizes. Many national parks such as the Cape Cod National Seashore in Massachusetts feature Class I bikeways. Wisconsin has a 300-mile mixed class bikeway through cities, towns, back roads, abandoned railroad beds, and the like. A number of towns make instant bikeways by closing parks to autos on weekends and selected weekday nights. A really enterprising town is Littleton, Colorado, which created 23 miles of bikeways. One side of the street is reserved and specially marked for two-way bicycle traffic. Cars are not even allowed to park on that side of the street, and violators get tickets. So do bike riders who disobey traffic regulations. The Littleton venture has been a great success (they should have about 50 miles of bikeways now), and inspired by this example other cities in Colorado – Boulder, Lakewood, Aurora, Denver, Englewood, Northglenn, Aspen, and Fort Collins – have either created or are creating bikeways.

Bikeways are a good idea. The Bicycle Institute of America, 122 East 42nd Street, New York, N.Y. 10017, will send you free a blizzard of information and workable plans for how to get bikeways in your community. Despite the fact that some bikeways are sheer tokenism distinguishable in no way whatsoever from a regular highway or street, there are some good ones, and the idea is sound, especially if you push for Class I and II bikeways. I hope that you will engage in such activity.

At the same time the shape of things to come may be a little hairier than Sunday rides with Mr. Lindsay. No major concessions will be made to cyclists as long as the automotive and petro-chemical industries hold the economic clout. A glimpse into the future has been provided recently in France.

Paris is famous for traffic. Cars are everywhere, moving in a constant rushing stream, and creating an incredible din. Cars have the right of way and pedestrians have to fend for themselves. In Paris the auto is King. Mr. Pompidou has even announced, "We must adapt Paris to the automobile and renounce a certain aesthetic idealism."

Not all Parisians agree. They want alternate means of transportation and an end to noisy traffic jams. On April 23, 1972, the organizations Les Amis de la Terre, Comité Anticuleaire de Paris, Comité de Liberation, Ecologique, Etre, Objectif Socialiste, and the Federation of Users of Public Transport staged a massive bike-in to dramatize their demands. It was beautiful.

Some 10,000 bicycles of every conceivable type and condition rendezvoused at Porte Dauphine. A few forward-looking Frenchmen showed up on roller skates! Harried police tried to route the demonstrators to exterior streets, but the procession went straight down the Champs Elysées to the Place de la Concorde, up the Blvd. St. Germain, and on to Bois de Vincennes (a park). Bus loads of riot police tried to stem the tide on the Champs Elysées but failed, possibly because they did not want to be violent in full public view. As the procession wound along replete with signs and streamers, some sympathetic motorists blocked side streets with their cars to add to the confusion, and pedestrians shouted "Bon Courage!" One spoilsport who refused to be stymied ran into several bicycles with his car. Surrounded by several thousand angry bicyclists he paid damages on the spot.

When the cyclists reached Bois de Vincennes, they were greeted with victory hymns by the Grand Magic Circus troupe. An hour of dancing, singing, and good times followed. Then the CRS riot police arrived. Helmeted troops on motorcycles charged the crowd and tear gas flew. Efforts at reason failed. About 50 people were arrested. The CRS used the shelter of the woods to smash up bicycles with their nightsticks.

Now Les Amis de la Terre and other groups are pressing on with their demands: the creation of pedestrian streets; one million free bicycles at the disposition of Parisians; non-polluting public transportation à la Rome; the closing of Paris to more automobile traffic, and a halt to the creation of inner-city expressways. *Yeah!*

The French experience points the way to real victories. Theirs was an *ecological* demonstration stressing the needs of both pedestrians and bicyclists. Bikeways are not enough. What is needed is the elimination of polluting transportation. In urban areas the car accounts for up to 85% of the air pollution, and for 85% of the noise pollution. The absolute elimination of internal combustion engines from urban areas is the practical solution which benefits everybody. The bicycle and roller skate are wonderful pollution-free adjuncts to such a campaign.

As the existence of good bikeways attests, it is not necessary to get tear gassed or clubbed in order to get something done. But the industries with vested interests in maintaining a motor age are large and powerful to the extreme. Petro-chemical companies are a law unto themselves. They routinely buy and sell governments. Steel, mining, rubber, textiles, cement, and plastics are automotive-related industries, each with a profit and make-work situation to protect. Each, curiously enough, is a major pollutor in its own right. Ultimately, the only solution to this vicious conglomerate of vested interest and power will be to take the profit out of their activities by nationalizing all transportation – bicycles, cars, trucks, buses, trains, airplanes – and all related service industries. In the technology-oriented U.S. of A. this is economic and psychological revolution.

What we are more likely to see is a long series of minor reforms, tokenism, and other concessions to public unrest. If we are lucky, there will be a major smog disaster in which thousands of people will suddenly die all at once, instead of piecemeal as they do now. This might spur improvements which would ultimately save more lives than were lost. But the power of vested interests in maintaining a motor age is such that there will probably be a long, drawn-out struggle, and concessions will not be won without a fight.

So don't be too surprised if you are beaned at a bike-in by a club-swinging cop who calls you a dirty communist, and don't back off because of it. *You have a right to live.* Arguments which present the roller skate or bicycle as more economical, efficient, etc. are all well and good, but the situation is extremely simple: present transportation systems are filling the air with deadly fumes and noise and recklessly wasting a dwindling supply of natural resources. *They are killing and injuring people.* You have a right to live – it is your birthright – but you will have to fight for it.

Do it!

Index